VIEW NORTH

VIEW NORTH

A Long Look at Northern England

FREDERICK ALDERSON

DAVID & CHARLES : NEWTON ABBOT

7153 4282 7

Printed in Great Britain by
Clarke, Doble & Brendon Limited Cattedown Plymouth
for David & Charles (Holdings) Limited
South Devon House Railway Station
Newton Abbot

CONTENTS

ACKNOWLEDGMENTS

The author wishes to acknowledge the help of the following authors, their agents or executors, and publishers, in giving permission for the inclusion in this book of short quotations of copyright material.

Edward Arnold Ltd for *British Social and Economic History*, by C. P. Hill; John Betjeman Esq for *First and Last Loves*, published by John Murray; Basil Blackwell Ltd for *Strikes*, by K. G. J. C. Knowles; Miss Sonia Brownell and Secker & Warburg Ltd for *The Road to Wigan Pier*, by George Orwell; Jonathan Cape Ltd for *Love on the Dole*, by Walter Greenwood, for *Pit-Yacker*, by George Hitchin, and for *Kilvert's Diary*, edited by William Plomer; Chatto & Windus Ltd for *The Uses of Literacy*, by Richard Hoggart; Rosica Colin Ltd for *Saturday Night and Sunday Morning*, by Alan Sillitoe; Dalesman Publishing Company for 'Red Rose, White Rose at Todmorden', by W. R. Mitchell; Gerald Duckworth Ltd for *A Hundred Years of Economic Development*, by G. P. Jones and A. G. Pool; Faber & Faber Ltd for *Redbrick University*, by 'Bruce Truscot'; Hodder & Stoughton Ltd for *Winter in England*, by Nicholas Wollaston; Michael Joseph Ltd for *Billy Liar*, by Keith Waterhouse; James Kirkup Esq for *A Spring Journey and Other Poems*, and for *Sorrows, Passions and Alarms*; Longmans, Green Ltd for *The Bleak Age* and *The Town Labourer*, by J. L. and Barbara Hammond; Manchester University Press for 'The Structure of Industry in Lancashire', by M. J. Pullen and B. R. Williams in *Manchester and its Region*; Penguin Books Ltd for *The Other England*, by Geoffrey Moorhouse; A. D. Peters & Co for *Oh Dreams, Oh Destinations*, by Phyllis Bentley, for *The Good Companions*, by J. B. Priestley, and for *Introducing the Arnisons*, by Edward Thompson; Laurence Pollinger Ltd for *It's A Battlefield*, by Graham Greene, and for *Lady Chatterley's Lover*, by D. H. Lawrence; Routledge & Kegan Paul Ltd for *Learning and*

Living, by J. F. C. Harrison; Stephen Spender Esq for 'An Elementary School Class Room in a Slum'; A. P. Watt & Son for *Clayhanger*, by Arnold Bennett, by permission of the owner of the copyright and Methuen & Company Ltd.

Apology is here tendered for any inadvertent omission in acknowledgment or failure to trace copyright holders.

ILLUSTRATIONS

The author's grateful thanks are due to the following individuals and concerns for illustrations used on the pages indicated.

G. Douglas Bolton, pages 49, 50; George C. Miller, page 113; J. A. Podmore, pages 61 (above), 62, 252 (below).

Blackburn Times, pages 63, 186 (above), 244; Burnley Borough Librarian, pages 242, 245; English Steel Corporation Ltd, pages 114, 115 (below), 128; Lilywhite Ltd, Brighouse, page 124; Macclesfield Borough Librarian, page 51; National Coal Board, page 254; *North Western News*, page 246; Radio Times Library, pages 177, 178, 180, 182 (above), 190, 192; Sheffield Newspapers Ltd, pages 59, 252 (above); *Shields Gazette*, pages 115 (above), 117, 126, 179, 181, 184, 189, 255; Stoke-on-Trent City Museum, page 127; Tolson Museum, Huddersfield, pages 64, 123 (above), 182 (below), 250; *Whitehaven News*, pages 118, 122 (above); *Wigan Observer*, pages 54 (below), 55, 119, 120, 121, 122 (below), 123 (below), 183, 241, 243, 247, 249, 256.

For the rest of the photographs, responsibility lies with the author.

PREFACE

A friend of mine, now a higher civil servant, was once persuaded
to accompany me on a walk along the course of Hadrian's Wall,
starting near Newcastle and finishing near Carlisle. Fresh from
his London public school and Cambridge, he had never ventured
into the 'barbarian' North before. To give himself confidence or
to provide protective camouflage or both, he bought a large
cloth cap and some strong plug tobacco for his pipe and sprinkled
his speech with 'bah gooms'. He was not a success. The native
Northerners merely thought what unaccountable barbarians these
Southerners had become, but were too polite to say so in his
hearing. Wherever he went with his cap and pipe and solecisms
of speech a hush fell upon the company, not of respect but of
surprise. So that's what Southerners are like away from their
native heath, we've always thought that they 'put it on', was the
verdict. My friend sensed somehow that his *persona* did not come
across and, as far as I know, he has never since ventured North
—which he called anywhere beyond the Wash.

So many of his background and similar places of upbringing
maintain the same attitude of separatism; which is a pity. A
friend from the Shires recently expressed to me more than
feigned anxiety about his possible reception in the North and
about the roughness of manners and conditions, prior to ventur-
ing there on a family holiday. He, like Arnold Bennett, felt the
North began at Stoke: though Bennett, it must be admitted,
called men from Lancashire and Yorkshire 'Midland types'.
After it was over the mingled pleasure and relief on his face
showed the extent of his surprise.

It is true that in some respects going North is like travelling
in a foreign country. The roadside halts are different. The pubs
have names like 'The Kicking Cuddy', 'The Pit Laddie', 'The
Mechanic', 'The Brass Man', 'The Alkali', 'The Engineer's Arms',
'The Miner's Arms', 'The Ship Launch', 'The Distressed Sailor',

'The Spinner's Arms'—names as idiosyncratic to the preoccupa-
tions and pursuits of their areas as 'Waggon and Horses', 'The
Woodman', 'The Hop-pole', 'The Haycock', 'The Barley Mow'
are to pastoral areas. At noon instead of a ploughman's lunch
with 'scrumpy' they may offer exhibition ale and mussels. It is
true also that the signs and notices sometimes refer to odd things
such as SLUBBING DYERS AND MELANGE PRINTERS, vacancies for
SKILLED GORE MAKERS or for DANDY ROVING TENTERS : that there
are raw meat and liver shops, 'everything for your pets', OPEN ALL
WAKES and TRIPE WORKS, and rows of houses with names like
BOBBIN STREET or CANTEEN STREET or INDUSTRIAL BUILDINGS,
while passages and alleys become snickets, jetties or ginnels.

Of course they form part of a different tradition, as does the
Lancashire cobbler who displays in his window the art of 'pin-
pointing'—designs of flowers, scenes and animals on soles made
with fine nails and various stains. Or the Cumberland clogger,
who sets out his steel- and brass-toed clogs, from largest men's
to smallest child's, in coloured rows like a toyshop and who talks
of the time before pit mechanisation when miners' needs kept
fourteen cloggers busy in one small town. Or the warm, oily,
heady smell of wool in bales that wraps one round in some West
Riding towns like an extra coat.

It may bewilder the traveller to be addressed variously as
'gaffer' or 'mate', 'hinny' or 'luv', 'man' or 'duck' by shopkeepers
male and female, as he moves round the friendly hinterland of
the North, but to be warned sharply GET IN LANE on entering the
county town of Lancashire. He may flatter himself on how
easily he is 'chatting up' the lunch-break workman on the park
bench and then, wishing to take his photograph, ask 'Will you
do me a favour?' and see the man's mouth tighten and a wary
glint come into his eyes. He may think the Yorkshire market
porter abrupt when, carrying a heavy load, he says to the stall-
gazers 'Move along there ladies . . . come on now, *shift* your-
selves'; or the Lancashire woman lacking in delicacy, when, being
asked the way, she replies 'Just round thur, luv, by th'backside
o' the church'. These are superficial signs that not all of England
has succumbed to uniformity or surrendered independence. Those

accustomed to textural smoothness elsewhere may find both stimulus and surprise if they go further in examining the fabric of the North, even shock on remembering that it *is* part of a greater whole, whose greatness it has largely made possible. If Northern readers find satisfaction looking for the faults or blind spots in one man's bird's-eye view of their territory, that expression of their interest will be enough.

As the study of industrial archaeology serves to record the physical mould of the early machine age, its mills and mines, foundries, canals and railways, so this patchwork survey tries to show the effect of the machine age on that part of the country and, above all, its people most directly involved. The context of the past is used to throw into relief features of the present. What was the landscape like in south-west Yorkshire, on Tyneside, in north Staffordshire, in south Lancashire before industrialisation began and again during its advance? What sort of people were those who became the factory hands, steel workers, engineers, managers, mill-masters and what influences, techniques and trade fluctuations left impress upon them? What opportunities had they to respond to the demands of progress, to education, leisure, religion, and what were the provisions made for their needs? To what extent do they or their attitudes differ from the rest of the populace, that the idea of separatism should arise? Has enough been done to put right the results of the industrial boom years, of plunder without planning, or has the muck stayed North as the money flowed South?

These are some of the questions asked. The answers, subject to the need for compression and the limits of individual impression, have been sought from personal memories, official reports, discussion and visits to the featured scene. Big cities—four of England's six biggest are in the North, although three of them show recent decline in population—take second place here to the smaller towns and cities, since cosmopolitan modes tend to obscure traditional idiosyncrasies. In the photographs, as in the text, it is the human background, the pattern of living which claims first attention.

One thing emerges clearly. The North is not nearly as black

as it is, or was, painted. Thanks to smoke abatement it is possible to enjoy a fine day in Sheffield or in Sunderland and to see across Burnley or Barnsley to the hills as seldom before, except during a period of strike. On Teeside, special instruments have now been installed to determine how much sunshine industry still shuts out, as distinct from natural haze. When the places mentioned or illustrated in this book were revisited about a year ago I linked them up by a camping tour. Each night for a couple of weeks tent was pitched on a site not more than four or five miles from a large industrial area and each site was in green and pleasant surroundings, often country of some grandeur. A few miles outside Sheffield there was a natural rhododendron valley equal to any in Wales or southern Ireland, with skylarks and fox-hounds, not hooters and lorries, for morning music. The air was fresh: 'wind's a bit thicky, isn't it?' said the passing postman. Two considerations occurred. One, that it was not widely enough realised how green and open most of the industrial North's 'out-back' is still: the other was that it should be kept so.

'Old growth areas fight for a new image, while the technology of the 1960s brings prosperity to towns which missed the scars of the nineteenth century'. An industrial correspondent of *The Times* is commenting on the fact that coalfields are no longer the main magnet of industry. The light industries, with grid power supplies, tend to 'home' South, round London, to the Midlands or to Severnside and new boom towns are on the way. The next revolution of the industrial wheel may make those scarred areas of the North, with their proximity to something more than 'green belts', places of envied retreat from the growth areas of the South or West. Wigan, where the tall brick façades of Wallgate glow as rosily pink in late sunshine as the Palace of the Winds at Jaipur, soon may acquire period appeal. In which case a wiser motto for the separatist now would be 'Integrate'.

LANDSCAPE

The cities are strewn across the North
Like mucky snags that grace a miner's back . . .
The North, Brian Higgins

Two hundred years ago, before collieries opened up on all
sides, it (Wakefield) *must have been a lovely little place in a*
beautiful countryside.
Yorkshire West Riding, Lettice Cooper, 1950

Between mid-eighteenth and mid-nineteenth century the im-
memorial aspect of rural England, east, south and west, was
transformed. The vast 'open fields' of each village, across which
Cromwell and Prince Rupert had been able to charge their
cavalry, and the surrounding 'waste land' of moor and marsh,
self-sown wood and coppice, were gradually changed by the
Enclosures into a chessboard of hedge, ditch and plantation, so
familiar today, which gave to the whole distant country 'the
appearance of a large and majestic garden'. Much of the North
and north Midlands was changed also, in the same period—from
green to black.

The industrial landscape of the North, as it has become,
generates a love-hate relationship with those who know it best.
With no pretence to charm, to gentleness, to gracious vistas, soft
retreats, it sets up a barrier in those who are bred upon it against
their ever being fulsome in praise of its special features, or ever
fully satisfied with landscape of any other sort. When they are
forced to work and live there they think, or say, they would
sooner live almost anywhere else : when they are free to do that
then they find they cannot 'settle' elsewhere. This northern landscape has power, drama, endurance, surprise, bad taste and a

sense of better days long past. It fits the people like a glove. It
has suffered the worst that industry can do and still retains a
various character and sharp identity, when that part of England
south of the smoke becomes every year less and less distinguishable from a cross between holiday camp and golf course. However appallingly treated by man, this landscape has the basically
fine lines, textures of stone and brick, counterpointing of chimney
and hillside, which continue to fascinate long after they have
ceased to shock or surprise.

The 'homing on' and proliferation of industry in the North
occurred for different reasons at different locations. When mills
were worked by water power they were set up in the upper
reaches of Pennine valleys, where streams flowed strong and
constant. (A few remain, still working, like the 'breast-fed' flax
mill near Pateley Bridge.) Then, as steam power ousted water
power, coal seams, coupled with supplies of soft water, became
the magnet for factory building in the woollen and worsted
trades. The southern part of the West Riding had almost a total
monopoly in worsteds. The cotton industry concentrated in south
and central Lancashire not only because cheap coal was at hand,
but because the damp climate of the Atlantic seaboard specially
suited cotton-spinning and there was the port of Liverpool, both
to handle imports of raw cotton and exports of manufactured
goods. Supplies of iron-ore, coking coal and water promoted the
great developments of steel trades in Sheffield and district:
Barnsley had been known as 'Black Barnsley' even in Defoe's
time from its 'smoaky aspect'. The presence of coal, limestone,
salt and suitable sand advanced the glass and chemical industries
of St Helens, Widnes, Northwich, Warrington. Coalfields and
ironstone underlie the concentration of metal works and potteries
in the Black Country, factories and houses in Burslem being
built on the coalfield itself. So the face of the north Midlands and
Northern England was changed primarily by what lay under it
—once scientific techniques were applied to the use of mineral
resources.

By 1790, the Black Country proper was no longer wild moorland but a land of forges, collieries, canals, with steep streets,

marl-pits, pot-banks, terraces, and derelict ground all in a con-
fused tangle. The cradle of the Industrial Revolution, Coalbrookdale, has a clearly blackened appearance in a print showing the
ironworks in 1805. The change wrought by industry in north-
west Durham earned comment in the *Universal Magazine*, 1788:
'Before, Winlaton (near the modern centre of the steel industry
at Consett) consisted of a few deserted cottages, but now contains
1,500 inhabitants, chiefly smiths.' The ironworks was already
supposed to be the greatest manufactory of its kind in Europe.
Collieries, wagonways and pitmen's cottages appreciably altered
the character of the countryside in west Cumberland. By 1800,
mining and shipment of coal had created the industrial towns of
Whitehaven, Workington, Maryport and there were other
colliery hamlets nearby.

As yet, the areas of change were restricted, but within another
generation or so the effects of a mounting demand for coal, iron
for railway development and of mining colonisation were to
become indelibly marked. In 1841 a member of the Children's
Employment Commission wrote of east Durham: 'Where
formerly there was not a single hut of a shepherd, the lofty steam-
engine chimneys of a colliery now send their columns of smoke
into the sky, and in the vicinity a town is called, as if by enchant-
ment, into immediate existence'. When railway building made
it possible for the Tees to enter the coal trade another port, besides
Stockton, the first boom town of the industrial revolution, was
soon required and a town adjoining the new shipping staiths was
created from scratch—Middlesbrough, whose first house went up
in 1830. Twenty years later discovery of ironstone nearby boosted
its growth. Its rigid grid plan gives the 'feel' of an early industrial
town. It possesses a zone known as the Ironmasters' District.

༺❀༻

MIDDLESBROUGH is obviously not a place that people would
be likely to settle in unless there were very practical reasons
for their doing so. There are no immediate surroundings, either
of buildings or of country, to appeal to the aesthetic side of
imagination. So late as 1801 it had only twenty-five inhabitants.

It was no larger, in fact, than the little hamlet of the same name which six or seven centuries before had stood on the banks of the Tees at a place where the monks going between Whitby and Durham were ferried across.

In 1811 the population of Middlesbrough was   35
In 1821   40
In 1831   154
In 1841 (after the railways had begun)   5,463

In 1850 the ironstone was discovered in the Cleveland Hills, ten miles from Middlesbrough, and then the great town rose on the banks of the Tees, within reach, on the one hand, of the Durham coalfields, and on the other of the Cleveland ironstone. There could not have been a more favourable place for an ironmaking centre.

The population in 1861, after the discovery of the iron, had risen to 18,892.

In 1871 the population of Middlesbrough was 39,284
In 1881   55,288
In 1891   75,532
In 1901   91,302

At the moment of writing the Municipal Borough is over 100,000.

At the Works: A study of a Manufacturing Town, Lady Bell, 1907

಩ಀಁ

On the Lancashire-Yorkshire borders the landscape's transformation was less sudden and to some extent held in check by the nature of the terrain. Formerly one of the most barren areas of England, Lancashire, in 1790, had a population of only 600,000—compared with the figure of 2,500,000 for five of its big towns today. In a work of fiction, published anonymously in 1860, *Scarsdale, or, Life on the Lancashire and Yorkshire Border Thirty Years Ago*, James Kay (later Sir James Kay-Shuttleworth), looked back to the appearance of this countryside during its transition. The landscape is viewed historically as well as geographically.

Whoever is familiar with the chain of hills which separates the counties of York and Lancaster is aware that its wild moors raised from 1,800 to 3,000 [*sic*] feet above the sea, feed streams watering valleys of great beauty on either slope of the desolate mountains. The narrower gorges of the upland valleys often have banks two or three hundred feet high, clothed with woods through which bluffs pierce too steep for the growth of timber, or where tall cliffs stand like pillars showing the lines of stratification amidst the alders, hazels and ivy which partially clothe their rugged and broken forms. Issuing from these glades and cloughs the Swale, the Wharfe, the Ribble, the Lune, the Aire, the Calder find wider vales with level meads called 'holms' or 'ings' covered with the brightest verdure. In the openings of such valleys, still within the shadow of embowering woods, the monasteries of Fountains, Bolton, Salley and Whalley show where cultivation won from the primeval forest its early and richest rewards. . . .

It is chiefly below the ruins of these abbeys that the fair virgin features of the valleys are scarred by manufactories. But the railway viaduct at Whalley bridges the Calder as high above the river's bed, just beyond the precincts of the abbey, as the Pont du Gard, with works of Roman simplicity and strength. The chimney of the loom-shed built at its foot scarcely rises above the level of the iron road. . . .

After the first print-works or cotton mills are passed, factory and hamlet regularly succeed each other. In a walk of a few miles the valley deepens; the slopes on either side become bare rocks, and at length, on one side (the traveller) passes beneath a wall of lofty crags, from the edges of which one of singular form beetles over, so like an eagle in act to spring from its eyrie into the air, that it is known as the Eagle's Crag. . . .

This is the valley of TODMORDEN, but at this very point a factory is built in a gorge where there is barely space for the road, the mill and the torrent between the crags and the opposite precipitous slope. Hence all down the valley to LITTLEBOROUGH and ROCHDALE, the bottom of one of the most picturesque gorges in England is choked with mills, loomsheds, manufacturing hamlets and villages in rapid succession : the railway, the canal and the road often occupying the whole level space of the hilly pass. Here and there the farmhouses on the slopes alternate with some small, old, stone mansion, with a quaint porch and over it a long window and an escutcheon with a motto and date.

Power, drama, endurance, surprise—the scene possesses these characteristics still. It is soiled, but never insipid, bleak, yet not uninspiring, challenging, not tame. 'Let no southerner for one moment imagine that the northerner is ashamed of his native heath : he does not envy them their climate, their comparatively unspoiled countryside or their culture.' The observation is just, but the taste for such landscape is an acquired one : it has grown upon this northerner not without his repining for the better days long past. Ruskin, writing within a year of Sir James Kay-Shuttleworth, told of driving the twenty miles from Rochdale to Bolton. The valley had been one of the most beautiful in the Lancashire hills, one of the far-away solitudes full of the old shepherds' ways of life. 'At this time there are not I think more than a thousand yards of road to be traversed anywhere without passing a furnace or a mill.' When we move on another hundred years and look at a similar stretch of country, the gulf between pastoral and industrial and the tastes formed upon them is fully manifest. 'From a hill-top near my home, above Bury and Bolton I once counted 127 mill chimneys spread through 180 degrees beneath me. It was during Wakes Week, the local holidays, and the chimneys were inactive, so that visibility was uncommonly good, and you could even pick them out faintly in the direction of Oldham and Rochdale too. At night, or in the winter after-noons, with three or four storeys of lights ablaze, they looked from a distance like a convoy of liners moving over the land' (Geoffrey Moorhouse). Not everyone can adjust to the effect of tranforming LANCASHIRE and YORKSHIRE into the leading work-shop of the world.

To appreciate the drama of this border country, the powerful congruity of wild moor, mill-stone grit and narrow valleys 'where like enormous dice, the grey, black-windowed mills are cast' the writer recommends a perambulation of that upland road, called on the Ordnance map, The Long Causeway. It leads from BURNLEY *via* Mytholm to HEBDEN BRIDGE, with Blackshaw and Heptonstall Moor to the north, the Calder valley, Forest of Rossendale and Todmorden to the south. The prospect may not wholly please, but it will nowhere disappoint. To come to close quarters with the moors themselves the hardy traveller may then proceed by HEBDEN WATER, Black Dean and Widdop Cross to COLNE, with Boulsworth Hill stretching away north (Lad Law, 1,700 ft) and immense wave-lashed reservoirs on every side. A late autumn evening over here can provide an unforgettable experience.

⚬⚬⚬

> The hills are sudden here; the crags and cloughs,
> The burnished woods and windy, deer-brown moors
> Wait to surprise : each narrow valley bluffs
> That no through road exists : or seen from towers,
> Crowning the heights like mill-less chimney stacks,
> Exits are lost in setts, old lanes and packhorse tracks.
>
> Calder Valley

The hill country has come out of the industrial assault best. Encroachment could go only so far, the barriers of moor and crag remain. The Pennines have baffled many intruders since Defoe. 'I do not remember that there was one Bottom that had any considerable Breadth of Plain Ground in it, but always a Brook in the Valley running from those Gills and Deeps between the Hills. I suppose we mounted to the Clouds and descended to the Water Level about eight times in that little part of the Journey' (across Blackstone Edge to Halifax). Parts of the border area may be thought to suffer from the interpenetration of factory with farmland and sameness,

> the grey neutral tint of every object, near or far off, on the way from Keighley to Haworth. The distance is about four miles and what with villas, great worsted factories, rows of workmen's houses, with here and there an old-fashioned farmhouse and out buildings, it can hardly be called country any part of the way. The road passes over tolerably level ground, distant hills on the left, a beck flowing through meadows on the right and furnishing water power to the factories built on its banks. The air is dim and lightless with the smoke.

Mrs Gaskell's complaint applies to a good many of the outliers radiating from industrial or engineering centres close to the Pennines. Some observers prefer the centre aspect itself.

⚬⚬⚬

> Across the valley thick with mills,
> The fellside rises like an aerial map
> Of fields and drystone walls and farms,

Pylons saunter over with a minimum of fuss
And round the bend from Keighley comes the Brontë bus.

Visit to Brontëland, James Kirkup

ᴄᴀᴍ

BURNLEY is beautiful for a passer-by, if you like steep streets and
viaducts with steam trains swinging over the mills and steel
bridges across a street that are as likely to carry a canal as a railway, and tall chimneys and hillsides coated with roof-tops and
church steeples standing like cypresses in the rain . . . and con-
trasts of every grey in a landscape where the only colour is in
the green that sometimes touches the stone as though the moorland moisture had induced a slime. (Nicholas Wollaston)

A more delicate harmony is achieved between the silk industry's
tall Regency mills of clear-pointed brick or stone with their moon-
like clocks in the pediment and the high surrounding hills and
moors of Macclesfield: in places chimneys and church towers
together accent an almost parkland scene. Everywhere, in fact,
the older industrial architecture, using local building material
and simple domestic forms, achieves a congruity which puts most
glass, steel, concrete and cantilever construction quite out of
court. The primitive, child-like style of factory building in parts
of Lancashire, black stone outlined by white mortar, tall
chimneys at the end of small gabled sheds, regular oblong shapes
and uniform windows, integrated effortlessly with the prim rows
of cottages, narrow connecting 'ginnels', and homely landscape.

In the aesthetics of this industrial landscape the eye of the
beholder and the climate of contemporary taste are all important.
Other things being equal, hill country and stone building provide
a satisfaction which plain and brick rarely can. 'The difference in
visual appeal between the textile belt of the West Riding and the
coalfield area of Barnsley, Doncaster, Rotherham where the hills
have petered out is already marked: isolated pockets of undulat-
ing pasture, trees and hedges among the slag heaps, mining sub-
sidence and dilapidated houses serve to emphasize the industrial
blight', (Moorhouse). One has only to travel by train from, say,
HALIFAX to ROCHDALE, or HUDDERSFIELD to MANCHESTER, climbing all the time in narrow cuttings and through curving crag-

crowned valleys with glimpses of golden-brown moor and with rows of old, dark, brown stone weavers' cottages ridged along the sides, to experience the feeling of deflation, almost depression when one emerges from the last long tunnel, drops swiftly down to flat levels and contemplates the wasteland of sooty brick and forlorn farmland that stretches seemingly for evermore into Cheshire. The journey reversed always promotes a corresponding lift in spirits. It is over these extensions of plain that industry recklessly sprawled and sprawled and houses were ribboned out until 'conurbation' has become the accepted pattern: one great concentration of human habitations stretches with hardly a break from south of STOCKPORT to the hill slopes north of BOLTON.

Conurbation of a comparatively restricted type can be seen in the north-east coastal plain between Tees and Tyne. Here coalfields, ironfields and the river estuaries led to intense industrial activity and dense settlement of population, especially during the second half of the nineteenth century, when railways had linked the ports to the mining hinterland. Expansion of the industrial sites, the needs of shipbuilding yards and the amalgamation of great shipping and engineering concerns, together with a population increase from 200,000 in mid-nineteenth century to 750,000 before the First World War, were the factors which produced out of the separate settlements of Tyneside a single elongated conurbation strung out along the tidal estuary. More recently the octopus of ICI has spread tentacles on Teeside also and during 1966-7 over £1,000,000 per week was being invested by industry there. Reaching from Tynemouth almost to the western edge of the coalfield, at Ovingham, the former ranks as one of the seven major conurbations in Britain, with a population of nearly 900,000 people. At its southern point, towards Cleadon, only two miles separate it from another conurbation at the mouth of the Wear. The greater part of these 'growths' consist of drab tracts of narrow, closely packed rows of working-class houses, built of brick and invariably slated, crowded in close proximity to the works.

The contrast between this north-eastern development and the north-western coalfield region is due partly to the Cumberland area's considerable remoteness from major national markets, its less extensive resources with the centres of coal production moving seawards, and therefore its less pronounced build-up in population. The fact, also, that whilst early economic development and coal production were of similar pattern in all its centres, the newer industrial developments have kept separate the functions of MARYPORT, WHITEHAVEN and WORKINGTON, with light industries, steel and chemical industries as their respective supplements to mining, has played an equally important part. With two market towns, COCKERMOUTH and EGREMONT within range, and with CARLISLE for administrative services, none of the three mining towns and ports has dominated its neighbours nor extended its activities to overlap and embrace them. Conurbation has not taken place here: the towns maintain equidistant margins and along the Ellen valley from MARYPORT to Mealsgate the collieries and pit terraces and mineral lines are interspersed with farmland. But, as the planners and statisticians warn us, if population in Britain should increase the expected fifty per cent by the end of this century many people will look to the North of England for a place to live and to earn a living and Cumberland, with its industrial renaissance after severe trade recession, should become 'one of the most promising growth areas in the country'.

ᛞᚹᛞ

The Northern Economic Planning Council is recommending to the Government that a study be made of the Carlisle Solway Basin with a view to its establishment as a major industrial area. Much will depend on the feasibility or not of a Solway barrage to provide the water and power.

The council also urges a substantial increase in the reclamation of derelict land in West Cumberland. It estimates that no fewer than 2,287 acres in all are derelict, through abandonment of industries, pit heaps, the depression of harbour areas etc. Of these it considers that 1,411 acres justify treatment; in 1965 only 34 acres were reclaimed or landscaped, while the plan for 1966 was for a further 113 acres to be tackled. It would be a reasonable aim to complete reclamation within ten years, but with further dereliction inevitably adding to the problem, a much increased rate of reclamation at about £1,000 an acre will be necessary.

Dereliction can be a strong psychological factor in such a marginal region. The appalling ugliness of parts of the Black Country for instance does not appear to inhibit the desire for further growth there. But, for example, the misery of MARY-PORT'S deserted dockland, and the disregard for amenity considerations in the WORKINGTON industrial area, are hardly conducive to the attraction of industries and the social developments that accompany them.

Under the 1966 Industrial Development Acts the whole of Cumberland is a designated development area.

The Guardian, 17 November 1966

∾᷅ᕕᕗᕗ

The appearance of the industrial landscape or 'townscape'—whether it is the bi-nuclear conurbation of Teeside based on Stockton and Middlesbrough, or the Merseyside twin conurbation of Birkenhead and Liverpool, the 'Two Cities' of Manchester, Salford and their satellites, or the 'Five Towns' of Stoke, or the West Riding woollen[1] group—first impresses the outsider with the similarity of its sprawling ugliness, rather than with those qualitative differences that lead him when he is settled there to say of almost any northern community that it has more identity than a southern town.

Most Northern cities and industrial towns appear purposive, built-for-the-job, solid like the underlying rock, not concerned to put on a show, nor to pretend that granite and concrete are the same thing, and equally impervious to convenience, embarrassment or aesthetics. Their personalities are as no-nonsense as were their early founders. Town-hall square or city centre in BRADFORD, BURNLEY, HALIFAX, HUDDERSFIELD, or for that matter BARNSLEY, CHESTERFIELD, BLACKBURN, SHEFFIELD will demonstrate this. As the official guide to one such town says, beyond a foreground of railway and rooftops, a middle distance of houses and factories—square-looking, utilitarian factories many storeys high—the lower town chimneys thrust into the sky 'for after all this is a great manufacturing town and factories must be accepted as an essen-

---

[1] The density of its population impressed Defoe, the sides of the hills being already 'spread with houses' around Halifax.

tial part of its character'. By contrast a Midland city, such as Worcester, surrounded by blossomy country, a fine river, a Malvern Hills skyline, has surprisingly little sense of character. Its cathedral facing a modern shopping centre, its half-timbered Shambles elbowed by car park and glass-and-concrete 'development', its Georgian houses and High Street of multiple stores, its pretty county cricket ground and dominating gasometer, remain incongruous, unassimilated elements in what might easily end as 'the biggest and ugliest supermarket in the whole Midland area', barely distinguishable from so many others further south. These elements add up to nothing nearly so positive as the heart of any mainly nineteenth-century Northern city, for all its blackness.

◦⚬⚬◦

The region of MANCHESTER has grown in size and importance until there are now some $2\frac{1}{4}$ million people living within ten miles of the city and $4\frac{1}{2}$ million within twenty miles : from such suburbs as Gorton, originally an independent urban district, but absorbed by Manchester in 1890, the endless rows of drab nineteenth-century workers' houses, 'brick boxes divided into four compartments', syphon smoke into the atmosphere.

It is easier to say what the conurbation is *not* rather than what it is. Greater Manchester it is not, for one of its main characteristics is the marked individuality of its numerous towns, such as BOLTON, BURY, ROCHDALE, OLDHAM and STOCK-PORT . . . Beautiful they may not be : interesting they most certainly are. They are not merely industrial satellites of MANCHESTER, but rather towns whose relation to Manchester is tempered by their rugged individuality of form and spirit.

Manchester and its Region, T. W. Freeman, 1962

◦⚬⚬◦

This sense of individuality, in a uniformly despoiled scene where the boom years spelt 'plunder without planning', is the residuum of place appeal stronger than beauty and often projected as a defence against official schemes for improvement. At elemental level it provokes outbursts like that of the scrap-metal sculptor from Liverpool who fears that the town planners will turn a city into a 'neon-lit mortuary', 'a dehumanised egg-box'

or 'hell on Merseyside', in their anxiety to create faster traffic
routes, car parks and office blocks. When once ways of life have
been forced into congested and ugly places, family and neighbourhood patterns are established: then these places acquire a
character that no factory-cum-garden estate can replace or
achieve. 'Housing-estate ghettos like Kirkby, all bloody soulless
and the people won't know what they once had till they've lost it.
Conurbation, commuter, environment! Yaaahhh!'

In contrast 'The DEEPLISH STUDY on improvement possibilities in a district of Rochdale' lays stress on improving the areas
of old houses—comfortable family houses in neighbourhoods of
marked character and community feeling—and providing as
many as possible of the neighbourhood amenities now taken for
granted in new housing estates. Improvement of the individual
house needs to be reinforced by a quite new environmental
improvement, creation of playgrounds, providing space off the
streets for cars, remodelling streets from which traffic can be
excluded, ridding the area of breakers' yards etc, landscaping
spare ground, removing sheds, broken fences and planting
trees: even bringing into use a disused canal towpath, a brook
on derelict land and opening up the area round the church,
have a total effect of making the community district more cared
for, convenient and desirable.

'It's not open enough. We seem to be enclosed in with no
breathing space', is the residents' complaint: 'There's no
greenery. I'd like to see some trees.'

HMSO 1966

Arnold Bennett professed to feel the same way about Bursley,
where, in spite of the architecture of the streets, ragged brick
work, walls finished anyhow with slag, uneven alleys, higgledy-
piggledy workshops and kilns, cottages clumsily made into factories and factories into cottages, everything slovenly, makeshift,
filthy—he saw a new facial character to admire.

On a little hill in the vast valley was spread out the Indian-red
architecture of Bursley, tall chimneys and rounded ovens, the
new scarlet market, the grey tower of the old church, the high
spire of the evangelical church, the low spire of the church of
genuflexions, and the crimson chapels and rows of little red

houses with amber chimney pots, and the gold angel of the blackened Town Hall topping the whole. The sedate reddish-browns and reds of the composition, all netted in flowing scarves of smoke, harmonised exquisitely with the chill blues of the chequered sky. Beauty was achieved and none saw it.

It may be noted also that Burslem (or 'Boslem') remains dialect conscious—a sign nowadays of individuality.

As foreground of this townscape, from the railway near Etruria, the writer recently observed a scene to challenge a new Turner. The rural picturesque turns almost insipid beside the industrial picturesque of old workings—with their mounds of white saggars, soot-black columns of isolated and abandoned chimneys, huge purplish tips of waste, metallic green pools and rusty dumps of car bodies, the wet curves of a rail track and the lock of a stagnant canal—as seen against a darkening autumn sky fitfully lit by distant flares of furnaces. Whatever they destroyed in their reckless haste for wealth, the hands of Bounderby and Gradgrind left behind a new Gothic subject for Art.

༼ຄ฿ຄ༽

The East Midlands study, made by the East Midlands Economic Planning Council, draws an enlightening analogy between the position of the region on the Derbyshire-Nottingham border today, and Birmingham and the Black Country in 1900. The population of the East Midlands industrial area, in the quadrilateral between DERBY, NOTTINGHAM, MANSFIELD and CHESTERFIELD, is much the same, in the same square mileage, as in the Black Country in 1900.

In the Black Country at that time, as in the East Midlands today, identifiably separate towns could be seen on the map. Today the Black Country is one continuous built-up area; by A.D. 2000 the East Midlands area will have much the same population as the Black Country now has. It is hard to see how present planning techniques can prevent as unsatisfactory a pattern repeating itself, with an urban region conglomerating into a sprawling conurbation.   The Observer, 4 December 1966

༼ຄ฿ຄ༽

Visitors thinking to condemn have found themselves praising other features of the industrial scene. BRADFORD, the 'Florence

of the North' becomes a monument to the Industrial Revolution
piled up with Victorian pride, its streets and factories 'all turned
a soft and velvety black', its Wool Exchange 'a Victorian gem'.
(Those who live there would no doubt prefer smoke abatement
and clean stone or the days when trout still swam in the beck.)
LIVERPOOL with 'the smudge of the Cathedral tower looking
faintly Hindu in the distance, the funnels and masts behind the
dock wall, the Gothic warehouses of Bootle, the gantries of Birkenhead, the stumps of the New Brighton tower' looks 'pretty
good' to Nicholas Wollaston and has a 'curious imperial quality'
in spite of the murk that hangs over its black buildings 'made of
something like coal'. (One could also swop parts of it with
Bombay's post-imperial worst and not notice the difference.) For
those who enjoy period atmosphere no doubt BURSLEM—with its
solid-columned town hall and equally solid Wesleyan church,
both apparently made of congealed soot, its huge, pillared, por-
ticoed, double-staircased Sunday School, its public library with
rash of statues and figure of Josiah Wedgwood, its hushed, sober,
mahogany-panelled public bar (all near the town centre) and its
vistas of crumbling courts and grimly monotonous terrace houses
end-blocked by slag heaps or bottle kilns (now the resort of
coloured workers)—also has much to offer, besides its acrid air.
Even one of those strange grim streets in MIDDLESBROUGH, formed
by the kilns, the furnaces, the bunkers, darkened by iron plat-
forms overhead between the kilns and the gantry, streets in which
'everything is dull red and uncouth shapes appear through the
smoke of a winter afternoon like turrets and pinnacles', may strike
a chord for the connoisseur of nineteenth-century iron towns that
were 'pillars of cloud by day, pillars of fire by night'.

◦◦◦

Trafford Park is a modern miracle. Thirty years ago it was
the country seat of a family whose line goes back to the ancient
British kings and whose name the area retains. Thirty years
ago its woodlands were chopped down to clear the way for
commerce and to provide soles for Lancashire clogs. The Hall
still stands though it now houses only dust and memories and
echoes. And the twin lions surmounting either side of the wide

flight of steps now survey, instead of lawns alive with guests, a
double railway track only six yards away, and, where the
drives once wound their serpentine paths through the woods,
the fungus of modern industry, huge engineering shops, flour
mills, timber yards, oil refineries, automobile works, repositories
for bonded merchandise, choke and foul the prospect. The river
that flows at the foot of the adjoining paddocks is changed
also; it now gives hospitality to ocean going shipping from the
seven seas, shipping whose sirens echo mournfully in the
night : a river no longer in name even, but the MANCHESTER
Ship Canal.

Love on the Dole, Walter Greenwood, 1933

⫷⫸

At the very beginning of the spread of industry Wordsworth
conceived the idea of an area like the Lake District as 'a sort of
national property in which every man has a right and interest
who has an eye to perceive and a head to enjoy'. He inveighed
against discordant change, whether caused by railway building
or plantations; but the North of England generally has had no
such protective advocate. It is ironically amusing to note now
the attempts of official guides to industrial towns, whose corporations wish to attract yet further industrial development, in
pressing the claims of their contiguity to places still of natural
beauty. WORKINGTON the 'gateway of industrial north-west
England' obviously claims a stake in the Lake District and also
in the Solway Plain 'an unspoilt area'—but for how much longer ?
HALIFAX 'concerned to have its somewhat grim appearance beauti-
fied with the greenery and colour of trees and flowers in its
streets' offers 'bus rides to surrounding beauty spots in summer
as a Corporation undertaking. GATESHEAD 'the largest county
borough on the main line between NEWCASTLE and London'
with plenty of room for industrial development prides itself that
the Team Valley Trading Estate 'the most modernly conceived
industrial development in the whole world' (and the first Govern-
ment-financed estate to combat depression), is in a 'beautiful rural
environment'. Bare pasture-land has been converted to a garden
city of factories! The BURNLEY countryside—and BURNLEY is
very keen to erect new factories as well as to dispose of some of

its vacant cotton mills—appears to extend to Bolton Abbey (in
Wharfedale), Skipton (in Airedale), Wycoller (beyond the Forest
of Trawden), as well as to Tarn Hows (Lake District)—*Official
Guide*.

ᏯᎳᏯ

Compensations

The North-east is both better and worse than it is painted.
There is industrial and urban squalor worse than the indus-
trialist urged to move his factory and family north could probably imagine—think of unpaved streets in mining villages—
but it is by no means universal and there are compensations
—superb beaches, magnificent hills and rivers and woods,
the splendour of Durham city, the classical elegance of Newcastle's Grey Street, the charm of many country towns and
relatively unspoilt villages.

Pit heaps, the prime horror, are a resource as well as a
problem. They can be reshaped into sports stadia and ski-slopes,
they are being used to remould the landscape giving, in time,
fresh fields, woods, and streams. Durham county, with a greater
share of dereliction than any other part of the country (and
more experience in dealing with it), has a 10-year programme to
remove all the major eyesores. If coalmining declines at the
predicted rate there will be no inland mines by the 1980s.
This will increase the problem but it will enable every trace of
the industry to be erased.

The Guardian, 26 November 1967

ᏯᎳᏯ

Well-intentioned as these claims are—to have it both ways is
a not uncommon wish—perhaps humour is the best way out of
the industrial landscape dilemma, when it cannot be savoured
for its own sake. The humour is at the Northerner's expense.

'The very name of Stradhoughton', Man o' the Dales (Keith
Waterhouse) has written, 'conjures up sturdy buildings of honest
native stone, gleaming cobbled streets and that brackish air which
gives this corner of Yorkshire its own especial piquancy. . . .

' "Dark satanic mills I can put up with," I would say, "they're
part of the picture. But when it comes to dark satanic power
stations, dark satanic housing estates and dark satanic tea
shops. . . ."

' "That's the trouble with you youngsters," said Man o' the Dales. "You want progress but you want all the Yorkshire tradition as well. You can't have both."

' "I want progress," I retorted, "but I want a Yorkshire tradition of progress."

' "That's good. Can I use that?" said Man o' the Dales.'

HOME

The people that be about the fornacis be very ille colorid.
                                        John Leland 1540

*As you walk through the industrial towns you lose yourself in
labyrinths of little brick houses blackened by smoke, festering
in planless chaos round miry alleys and little cindered yards.*
                The Road to Wigan Pier, George Orwell, 1937

*Thank God I don't live up here: it's like going from heaven
to hell.*
                        RIBA Conference Report, 1963

The face of Northern England was fated to change from that
moment early in the eighteenth century when Abraham Darby,[1]
son of a Dudley Quaker, first applied his system of smelting iron
from coke instead of from charcoal. The change began at Coalbrookdale ironworks in Shropshire, but soon coal became the
magnet of industry everywhere.

Coal began the change: machinery accelerated it. The flying
shuttle for weaving, invented in 1733 by John Kay of Bury; the
spinning jenny invented by James Hargreaves of Blackburn; the
large water-propelled spinning frame of Richard Arkwright of
Preston; the spinning mule of a Bolton weaver, Samuel Crompton—these spelt approaching doom for cottage work with spinning
wheels. More than any other invention the power-driven water
frame was the prime cause of the change. It needed only James
Watt's application of steam instead of water-power, the rotary
engine of 1781, and the great switch from hand to machine, from
home to factory, from country to town was all but accomplished.

---

[1] 'Dud' Dudley discovered how to make iron with 'pit-cole' in 1619, but
his discovery died with him.

South Lancashire, it could be said, virtually invented the Industrial Revolution. Ironically it was local invention that turned local conditions upside down—as also with the stocking frame at Nottingham. The scale and speed of such change upset all plans and calculations for decent living conditions in industrial towns.

The state of the towns radically altered within two generations. Machine-run factories, attracting vast numbers of workers, countrymen, poor Irish and paupers as well as skilled tradesmen, concentrated them largely in the iron and coalmine areas. Whereas towards the end of the eighteenth century the number of country labourers was still double that of town workmen, before the middle of the nineteenth the situation was reversed. Town workers exceeded country by two to one, many of them being former English peasants used to an open-air life, in touch with the gentler rhythm, natural peace and beauty of the fields and woods. From being a quiet old market town Rochdale had swollen into a noisy straggling city; Birmingham had the appearance of a squalid village afflicted with elephantiasis. The process was progressive. In 1911 it was calculated that eighty per cent of the population of England and Wales lived in urban districts; moreover, within the previous forty years the total population of the country increased by almost half. This sudden disparate growth was the root cause of the industrial slums.

BURNLEY, for example, already a woollen and linen centre in 1700, then looked like any other small, prosperous market town with a central market cross, stocks, church, inn, smithy and prison for a population of about 2,000. A hundred years later the figure was 4,840, after which a population 'explosion' brought it to 21,000 within the next fifty years and 97,000 at the end of the nineteenth century. Some forty mills were erected during the first phase of that explosion. But, as commonly happened, apart from the old handloom weavers' cottages built high up the valley sides for the sake of daylight, the workmen's houses were crowded down among the mills; small, back-to-back, insanitary.

MACCLESFIELD, noted for its silk, button and twist manufacture, had a population of about 7,000 and eight streets of houses when Charles Roe introduced silk machinery and set up the first 'throwing factory' in 1756. Barely a lifetime later there were 150 streets, but as the official guide remarks 'the old charters of the town made no provision for dealing with such questions as sewage disposal, roads, lighting, water, health.'

HALIFAX—'Hell's cauldron' even to its best friends, owing to the multitudinous mill chimneys that shot up from the huddled buildings and poured out a heavy mist of smoke, soot and grime over the narrow valley—jumped from about 8,800 inhabitants to 28,000 in an even shorter period.

The rate of growth in many Northern towns—Leeds, Bradford, Bolton, Blackburn, Oldham—was as great or greater (the Leeds population, for example, grew from 53,000 to 123,000 between 1801 and 1831), and in them, a large proportion of their inhabitants had changed home, occupation and familiar surroundings. They had passed from the life of the village straight into the life of the slum.

'A low and grovelling mode of living' summed up the Poor Law Commissioners' view of town conditions during the first years of Queen Victoria's reign.

> The family lived in a cellar in Berry Street, off Stove Street: it was unpaved: women from their doors tossed household slops of every description into the gutter: heaps of ashes were the stepping stones. They got to some steps leading down to a small area, where a person standing would have his head about one foot below the level of the street: you went down one step even from the foul area into the cellar where a family of human beings lived. It was very dark inside. The window panes many of them were broken and stuffed with rags . . . the smell was so foetid as almost to knock the men down. Three or four little children were rolling on the damp, nay wet brick floor, through which the stagnant, filthy moisture of the street oozed up: the fireplace was empty and black. The wife sat in her husband's lair and cried in the damp loneliness. [His] fever was, as it usually is in Manchester, of a low, putrid, typhoid kind, brought on by miserable living and filthy neighbourhood.[1]

This picture by Mrs Gaskell is painted in the harsh tones of

[1] Cellar-dwellings were generally the resort of the immigrant Irish whose low standard of living and habits created problems similar to those of Northern cities today with concentrations of Pakistani or Jamaicans in their seedier areas.

cotton famine conditions. It seemed no less appalling to the eye
of Friedrich Engels when he was studying the proletariat of
South Lancashire, in the 'classic home of English industry and
masterpiece of the Industrial Revolution'. At Ancoats, he found
ragged women and children living in ruinous cottages, behind
broken windows mended with oilskin, sprung doors and rotten
doorposts, or in dark wet cellars in measureless filth and stench.
'In each of these pens containing at most two rooms, a garret and
perhaps a cellar, on the average twenty human beings live.' He
estimated that 7,000 people were served by only 33 lavatories.
The cellar population of MANCHESTER was 18,000 during the 40s.

⌒⌾∾

There are actually some property owners who are not
ashamed to let dwellings such as those which are to be found
below Scotland Bridge. Here on the quayside a mere six feet
from the water's edge is to be found a row of six or seven
cellars, the bottoms of which are at least two feet below the
low water level of the IRK. (The owner of) the corner house
above Scotland Bridge actually lets the upper floor although
the premises downstairs are quite uninhabitable and no attempt
has been made to board up the gaps left by the disappearance
of doors and windows. This sort of thing is by no means uncommon in this part of MANCHESTER, where owing to the lack
of conveniences, such deserted ground floors are often used by
the whole neighbourhood as privies.

The Condition of the Working Class in England, Friedrich Engels, 1845
(trans Henderson and Chaloner)

∾⌾⌒

The cholera epidemic of the 30s, which so alarmed the general
public, frightened the Government into a full-scale enquiry about
the labourers' lot in the new towns. They found a state of affairs
as dismaying as it was degrading.

The workers who were creating the industrial prosperity of
England were housed not so much in towns as in barracks.

Employers of factory labour had encouraged swarms of workmen to flock to industrial centres and speculative builders had

seized their opportunity. When they bought an acre of ground it was without reference to drainage, or any amenity, just the percentage return they could get for their money by placing as many houses on each acre as they possibly could.

BRADFORD's suburbs, for the most part, sprang up in this way : houses only half a brick thick, built back-to-back, without ventilation or drainage, and like a honeycomb, every particle of space occupied. They covered a superficial sixteen yards, cost less than a hundred pounds to erect and let at two or three shillings a week. Double rows of the houses formed courts, with a pump at one end and privy at the other—common to the occupants of about twenty dwellings. 'The workmen's houses at the bottom of the valley—BRADFORD lies on a little pitch-black, stinking river—are packed between high factory buildings and are among the worst built and filthiest in the whole city', said Engels. There were exceptions where large town landowners enforced the building of wide streets and good straight roads, as in BARROW-IN-FURNESS, HUDDERSFIELD and GLOSSOP. Maximum accepted standards in many areas would not meet the minimum requirements of BARROW, where housing and industry did not become inextricably mingled, a benefit still evident. Streets originally planned to be wide and airy, however, sometimes had a second row of houses wedged into them back to back, as happened to CHORLTON-ON-MEDLOCK.

⚜

Engels considered HUDDERSFIELD the most beautiful of all the factory towns in Yorkshire and Lancashire by reason of its situation and style of building, but still found whole streets, courts and alleys unpaved, unsewered, undrained. ASHTON-UNDER-LYNE seems to have merited second place, the factories being located close together on the valley bottom and the houses built away from them on the hill slopes.

⚜

Luckiest were those labourers whose lot fell in the time and the place where a unique mill-owner and philanthropist, like Sir

Titus Salt, built for his workpeople a model town, with baths and wash-houses, almshouses and infirmary, library and school, containing twenty-two streets of houses each with its parlour, kitchen, pantry and three or more bedrooms to accommodate families of different sizes, as well as an enclosed back garden. SALTAIRE remains basically unchanged after being about a century ahead of its times in planning . . .

The worst conditions of over-crowding afflicted those who had to live in the old quarters of existing towns—LEEDS, LIVERPOOL, MANCHESTER, NOTTINGHAM. In NOTTINGHAM, dense with lace and hosiery workers (although the inventor of a machine to make lace, John Heathcoat, was driven out of Nottingham, the spinning frame inventors, Arkwright and Hargreaves, expelled from Lancashire by angry workers, set up there instead), out of 11,000 houses over 7,000 were back-to-backs. Crowded in confined courts and alleys, sometimes even built side to side, they could be approached only through tunnels a yard wide, eight feet high and up to thirty feet long. BIRMINGHAM can still show some in use.

⁓⚬⁓

The factual drawbacks of living in quarters such as Holbeck, LEEDS are mildly stated by a United Domestic Missionary in his report of 1858 :

They (cottage houses) are built back to back, with no possibility of good ventilation, and contain a cellar for coals and food, the coal department being frequently tenanted with fowls, pigeons or rabbits, and in some cases with two or three of all these—a room from 9 to 14 feet by from 10 to 12 or 14 feet, to do all the cooking, washing and the necessary work of a family, and another of the same size for all to sleep in. Think for a moment what must be the inconvenience, the danger both in a moral and physical sense, when parent and children, young men and women, married and single, are crowded together in this way, with three beds in a room, and barely a couple of yards in the middle for the whole family to dress and undress in.

Learning and Living, J. F. C. Harrison, 1961

'A reckless and wanton invasion of property and liberty' thundered *The Times* when a Bill for regulating such housing was first mooted. Later, when the Bill was brought in, there came a change of tone : 'A town of manufacturers and speculators is apt to leave the poor to shift for themselves to stew in cellars and garrets'.

It might, of course, be said that it was not contractors but circumstances that were to blame—industry too rapidly mechanised, towns grossly swollen to meet factory demands, country-men turned into townsmen before they knew how to make their living conditions tolerable or before anyone else took that responsibility. What other causes were there for the unhappy poor to stew in cellars and garrets besides the prevalent vacuum of builders' conscience?

Firstly, there were no building restrictions in force.

> . . . there was in force a Window Tax for every window over eight : and so privies, closets, passages, cellars, roofs were left without.
> There was no refuse disposal system, sometimes not even a midden. In the north Midlands, Sunderland, Newcastle the idea prevailed that the heap when sizeable enough could be sold to a farmer—for profit! (Dickens in *Our Mutual Friend* has ironic comment on such huge, mysterious heaps : *vide* 'The Golden Dustman'.)
> There was no proper sewerage system : old sewers meant to carry off surface water into rivers were not suited for house refuse. When so used they caused huge, noisome cesspools often in the heart of the town itself.
> Street cleaning as a municipal obligation was a very slow starter. LEEDS at this period cleaned only 68 out of her 586 streets. SALFORD, ROCHDALE, PRESTON, LIVERPOOL had 'notional' cleaning once a week, but this did not include courts and alleys, the worst spots.
> Finally, fresh water was in as short supply as fresh air. It had either to be fetched from pump or standpipe, turned on for an hour or two weekly, or bought by the bucket from carts. This might cost a family two shillings a week.

Baths? For the poor? Available in polluted river or canal : otherwise dismissed as part of the increase of luxury and love of cleanliness which marks the present day.

Not all Northern towns mushroomed so chaotically in the same forty or fifty years. CHESTERFIELD, a town which claims to be the centre of industrial England, owed its great development to the rich seam of coal encountered by George Stephenson when he was laying the railway line to run through it. JARROW's population increased nearly ninefold in the forty years after Palmer's shipyard was started in mid-century and the first iron-screw collier and iron-clad warship had been built. For WORKINGTON, Cumberland, the discovery there of non-phosphoric pure iron ore needed for the steel process invented by Sir Henry Bessemer in 1856 was the decisive factor of growth. BARROW, ten years earlier than this a village of 325 souls, became a highly industrialised community of 70,000 people within the century for a similar reason.

The onslaught of industry which followed discovery of mineral wealth, in ironstone or coal mines, had characteristics unlike any other form of commercial enterprise. The district was suddenly swamped under a great rush from all parts of the country of people of the roughest kind to swell the ranks of unskilled labour. (For the majority of iron-workers the main equipment needed was health and strength—not deft hands, but strong arms.) The workmen all wanted to be as near as possible to their work, to waste no time or money in transit. They must have houses built as quickly and cheaply as possible, as big and no bigger than a workman's needs. So there sprang into existence a community of a pre-ordained kind: rows and rows of little brown streets, crowded together with no open spaces round them, with nothing spent on what was merely agreeable to the eye or even on what was merely sanitary, with no laying out a district into ideal settlements. When communities on this pattern, such as MIDDLESBROUGH, came into existence at once from the top to the bottom with no older nucleus or tradition, they were bound at the start to be rough-hewn.

Whatever the time-range of increase of population the time-lag in improving housing conditions was almost everywhere the same. Throughout the 1840s England was mad about railways, not about housing and health: but if the new English town was a raw settlement, where people lived as they do on a goldfield, at least it *was* a goldfield, for some.

Disraeli did his best to stir public feeling with a searing account of a Black Country town, which he called Wodgate (based upon an actual district near BIRMINGHAM):

> As you advanced, leaving behind you long lines of little dingy tenements, with infants lying about the road, you expected every moment to emerge into some streets and encounter buildings bearing some correspondence in their size and comfort to the considerable population swarming and busied about you. Nothing of the kind. There were no public buildings of any sort; no churches, chapels, townhalls, institute, theatre; and the principal streets in the heart of the town in which were situate the coarse and grimy shops, though formed by houses of a greater elevation than the preceding, were equally narrow and if possible more dirty. At every fourth or fifth house, alleys seldom above a yard wide and streaming with filth, opened out of the street. These were crowded with dwellings of various size, while from the principal court often branched out a number of smaller alleys or rather narrow passages . . . amid gutters of abomination and piles of foulness and stagnant pools of filth.

In MANCHESTER, back-to-back house building was forbidden by law in 1869, but in many other places speculators flouted the idea. In BRADFORD muck and money went together; and if it was money for only one class of people and muck for the other. . . . In the late 80s and 90s elective county councils were given control of local affairs such as housing and the Housing of the Working Classes Act (1890) was passed to stem the tide of slum dwellings. In practice, however, committees were easily packed by small capitalists and jerry builders, who could control the framing and supervision of by-laws about building and sanitation which, by the intention of Parliament, were to have controlled them.

❧

In BRADFORD in 1892 Jowett, the ILP representative, found that the majority of working people still lived in the same sort of houses as the one in which he had been born twenty-eight years before—one room upstairs, one room downstairs and a windowless cellar. Coal was kept in a portion of this cellar and the only form of sanitary provision was the privy midden (one to every four or more families). The houses were built back to back in long streets intersected by passages—the perfect environment for disease, squalor, and high mortality rates.

The writer's mother, a student teacher in BRADFORD, a year or two later than this, not surprisingly contracted typhoid fever.

⌇∞⌇

BRADFORD with its population of over a hundred thousand, fourth largest commercial centre in England, for long years held the palm as the 'most filthy town of the north'. The city's battle against squalor was costing it a mere £3,000 at a time when Railway Bills were being passed through Parliament for the raising of £300,000,000. The old rhyme does not discriminate in such matters:

> BRADFORD for cash, HALIFAX for dash,
> WAKEFIELD for pride and poverty,
> HUDDERSFIELD for show, SHEFFIELD what's low,
> LEEDS for dirt and vulgarity.

If the criterion had been street conditions perhaps the palm would have been shared with LEEDS or equally with LIVERPOOL. 'Ragged bare-footed women and children, enormous wealth and squalid poverty, wildernesses of offices and palatial counting houses and warehouses' as a visitor from Hereford, the Rev Francis Kilvert, noted in his diary during 1872. In a close-packed area down by the docks the mean streets built in his day were characteristically named after Victorian novelists and poets, their heroes and heroines. Over thirty of them can be counted on an old plan—Dombey, Dorrit, Pecksniff, Rokesmith, Wilfer, Wrayburn, Micawber, Nickleby, Pickwick, Maud, Enid, Elaine, Merlin, Mordred, Geraint, Gwendoline, Claribel, Shallot— Tennyson, Thackeray, Hemans, Shelley, Arnold, Wordsworth, Greenleaf (*sic*) and Whittier. Mill Street and Bessemer Street almost seem like uninvited guests in that company!

Kindly corners, of course, there were—and are—as exceptions to the squalid conditions brought about by the 'satanic mills'. Among the 'intakes', ground wrested from the grasp of

the moor between the industrial agglomerations of Lancashire
and Yorkshire—where even the towns seem at times only a
blacker edge to the moorland, outcroppings of its rock in the
form of hosts of chimneys and rows and rows of houses of blackening stone like ridges to the hills—in the 'cloughs' or narrow side
valleys or on the windy heights, people lived in independent
communities retaining the nature of a tight, snug, sturdy village.
CLIVIGER and CORNHOLME, COWLING and CONONLEY, OAKWORTH
and OXENHOPE; LUDDENDEN, RIPPONDEN and MARSDEN, MELTHAM,
MYTHOLMROYD; ALMONDSBURY, SOWERBY and SLAITHWAITE;
HAWORTH, HARDEN and HEBDEN BRIDGE, these and other places
still contrive to make home sound a homely, friendly spot. As close
to the bilberry moors and curlew-wheeling hills as to the vats and
frames and looms of textile manufacture, they are places where

> Over the Lowry landscape, backstreet piled
> On backstreet, pub, dam, river, factory gate
> And gabled Zion, blue mist floats, but wild
> The view and air of twelve hills, matching state
> For working lives whose wingéd thoughts have been
> Mount Tabor, Godly, New Delight and Tripping Green.[1]

⟶⟵

The buildings of Todmorden lie tight-pressed : they jostled
for whatever land was spare when road, canal and railway had
claimed the best strips.

Land slopes steeply to the wild, still virtually untamed region
of the Pennines, here thatched with ling. Two terms are used
locally : 'uplands' for the grassy parts, the high pastures ribbed
with walls and dotted with ancient-looking farms, and 'moors'
for the heathery bits, where peat layers are thick and black.

You can stand on some of these high places, only a mile or
so from Todmorden, without being aware of the town. Mills,
terraced houses, Victorian-looking shops, old pubs, railway
viaducts, and the weed-fringed canal are out of sight, deep in
the valleys. You look, instead, across the high Pennines, where
the ridges are like waves in a petrified sea, and the only really
prominent features are memorials like that on Stoodley Pike.

The Dalesman, W. R. Mitchell, 1967

⟶⟵

[1] Names of hamlets near the Calder valley.

It was not the provisions of local by-laws but the direct action of individual conscience that produced the first improvements in the homes and living conditions of the working classes. 'Slumming' or 'Poor peopling' by the wives and daughters of the well-to-do was an early, if not always welcome, form of this. Appeals to pity and sentiment by poets and writers was another. Elizabeth Barrett Browning pleaded support for the 'ragged schools' for children, or even a pause in the day's work to pray for those who

> All day drag their burden tiring
> Through the coaldark underground,
> Or, all day, drive the wheels of iron
> In the factories round and round.

Others interested themselves in clubs for the women who had to earn their bread by the sweat of their brow, needlewomen, match girls or factory workers—something more human than the basket of tracts and purse of shillings handed out by squeamish do-gooders.

Anthony Trollope declared that the real need was less separation between 'Lowtown', vulgar, dirty and devoted to manufacturing purposes, where troops of girls would be seen passing twice a day in their ragged, soiled mill dresses, and 'Uphill' where Paragon Crescent had been built by a man clever enough to see that as mills were made to grow in the low town, houses for wealthy people ought to be made to grow in the high town.

These sporadic efforts were only sops. Real progress went lame-footed until the sons of old and established capitalists began to devote themselves to the service of the public—with a provincial, aggressive and democratic impatience of parliamentary debate, decorum and privilege. Joseph Chamberlain, dapper Brummagem hardware merchant, showed the way. Those living on private wealth inherited under a *laissez faire* system could mitigate the evils wrought by it upon their employees. In doing so, of course, they helped to maintain the prestige of their class by appeasing social unrest. BIRMINGHAM, of which city Chamberlain became mayor in 1873—and where the more modern courts were kept 'tolerably respectable', the cottages far less crowded than in Manchester and Liverpool, by Engel's standards— enforced the Public Health Acts. Building and sanitary reforms were brought in to reduce the death rate, local services such as lighting, drainage, baths received attention: Corporation Street was cut through some of the city's worst slums. Slowly home conditions, under which the average age of death could stand in BRADFORD at twenty years, and the death rate of infants under five remain in MANCHESTER 57 out of every 100, were forced to the notice of Victorian complacency. Gadfly attacks upon industrial squalor by William Morris and by Ruskin kept the public conscience uneasy. Even so, to take a key example, the building of the retrograde back-to-back houses was not made illegal by general law until 1909.

Prohibition of back-to-back houses.

(1) Notwithstanding anything in any local Act or by-law in force in any borough or district, it shall not be lawful to erect any back-to-back houses intended to be used as dwellings for the working classes, and any such house shall for the purposes of this Act be deemed unfit for human habitation :

Provided that nothing in this section shall prevent the erection or use of a house containing several tenements in which the tenements are placed back to back, if the medical officer of health for the borough or district certifies that the several tenements are so constructed and arranged as to secure effective ventilation of all habitable rooms in every tenement.

(2) This section shall apply to any house commenced to be erected after the third day of December, nineteen hundred and nine, except that it shall not apply to houses abutting on any streets, the plans whereof were approved by the local authority before the first day of May, nineteen hundred and nine, in any borough or district in which, on the third day of December, nineteen hundred and nine, any local Act or by-laws were in force permitting the erection of back-to-back houses.

Housing Act, 1957

Whitestone and blacklead were popular working-class contributions to home betterment. When there were at all reasonable means of living in decency and cleanliness people in the manufacturing towns were as houseproud as any—excluding, that is, the Irish, whose standards even cellar dwellings did not lower. Yorkshire and Lancashire housewives kept their floors and steps washed clean, the step edges whitened or 'yellowed' with special hearthstone—on Tyneside they reddened them with 'bloodstone' —regardless of the fact that the first feet entering from the street would sully them again. Often twice a week steps, window-sills and the flag-stones in front of their doors received full treatment, women, girls and children kneeling on all fours with bucket, cloth and rubbing stone at their sides, until from a distance the pavements took on the appearance of a patchwork quilt. Neighbour vied with neighbour over the whiteness of the week's washing, even when furnace soot would soil it before it could dry. Hearth and fireside sparkled with polished brass knobs and black-leaded grate and oven; in front of it would be a thriftily made rag rug composed of scraps from old trousers and coats, cotton shifts or old stockings. No one could fault such housewives in 'fettling' (cleaning) when they were fairly housed. BURNLEY with its 50,000 looms and 500,000 spindles had the reputation of a place where household cleanliness ran neck-and-neck with godliness. In LEEDS one of the complaints of the poorer class was of the smoke that destroyed their tiny window gardens.

Manufacturers also lived by their mills in the Georgian and early Victorian era of most Northern industrial towns. In 'Milton' where the air tasted of smoke and a deep lead-coloured cloud that perpetually hung overhead was seen from miles around:

Mr Thornton lived close to the mill: the factory lodge-door at the end of the long dead wall was like a common garden door. It admitted into a great oblong yard, on one side of which were offices, on the opposite an immense many-windowed mill, whence proceeded the continual clank of machinery. On one of the narrow sides of the oblong was a handsome stone-coped house —blackened, to be sure, by smoke, but with paint, windows and steps kept scrupulously clean. It was evidently a house which had been built some fifty or sixty years.

The yard was but a dismal lookout for the sitting-rooms of the house. It seemed as if no one had been in the drawing-room since the day when the furniture was bagged up. The window curtains were lace : each chair or sofa had its own particular veil of netting or knitting. Great alabaster groups occupied every flat surface, safe from dust under their glass shades. . . . Peculiar cleanliness was required to keep everything so white and pure in such an atmosphere.

When company is expected Mrs Gaskell goes on to describe this apartment blazing forth in yellow silk damask and a brilliantly flowered carpet. Every corner is filled up with ornament, a striking contrast to the bald ugliness of the great mill yard and the dark shadow cast down from its many storeys.

At the second stage of their fortunes, in later Victorian times, although mill-owners did not leave the manufacturing town, they built solid stone mansions, with gravelled drives and stained glass halls, on some leafy height away from the worst smoke. On a more modest level, that of the partner in a small textile firm, the type of town house is described by Phyllis Bentley :

Thornleigh (in Halifax) was a solid, though not large semi-detached house, with a small steep garden at the front, a glass greenhouse at the side, and a large square yard at the back. Brown varnished Venetian blinds caused perpetual struggles of parallelisation in the dining-room where large bronze horses in rampant attitudes flanked a large bronze clock on the mantel-piece, and the dining-table was covered with a cloth of crimson chenille. The drawing-room at the back was all pale yellow silk and moss-green upholstery; it was much admired. There were large attics and, of course, equally large cellars. In the kitchen were two excellent maids . . . Everything at Thornleigh was essentially proper, essentially respectable, essentially middle-class. The house was spotlessly clean in every corner.

The inheritance is recognisable. Nowadays, or since the 30s, descendants of manufacturers and mill owners hark away over the moors to expensively converted farmhouses or split-level ranch dwellings, if they have not already settled for an Ilkley, Harrogate, Wilmslow or Wetherby type of commuting, while their mansions survive, if at all, as nursing homes, private schools or flats.

Whatever was done about homes fit for workers to live in by those town and city authorities that followed Birmingham's example happened tardily. There were various reasons—such as the one put forward at LEEDS for not forbidding back-to-backs in the beginning—that such house property was a favourite investment of small men : 1,200 freeholders had bought them out of savings. (The writer's grandfather was one such investor : some of his cottage property has only come under Clearance Order within the last year.)

Those who knew the industrial scene intimately did not conceal their disgust and impatience at the mess surrounding the homes of work people. Arnold Bennett comments after a return visit to the Five Towns in the pre-war years on the 'untidiness : things left at loose end : broken walls : deserted entrances : curious enclosed "ash-court" place : pit shafts, one only fenced in : men in bright neckties sallying forth : mean stunted boy crouching along smoking a pipe which he hid in his hand while holding it in his mouth : girls with heads wrapped up in cotton against powdery workshops : extremely foul and muddy road : smell coming from house. . . .' D. H. Lawrence in the 20s lashes out at the 'long squalid straggle of Tevershall, the blackened brick dwellings, the black slate roofs glistening their sharp edges, the mud black with coal dust, the pavements wet and black. It was as if dismalness had soaked through and through everything. The Wesleyan chapel was of blackened brick and stood behind iron railings and blackened shrubs : the church was away to the left among black trees'.

LEEDS in the 30s seemed to John Betjeman not very overcrowded, merely appallingly badly housed with infant mortality, tuberculosis and results of 'compulsory constipation' still alarming. He saw the same negation of the natural urge for beauty and gladness in life as was seen by Lawrence. If not so depressing the old house planning would have been comic.

At the east end of the town the houses were built close up against the factories for the workers : rows of two-storey houses with only the cobbled street and houses opposite to look at.

Several families lived in each two-roomed house. Go to the bottom of Nippet Lane and see what the old speculators did. A man named Weller bought a small bit of ground. On it he crammed as many houses as possible, running in straight lines off the main street; Weller Avenue, Weller Grove, Weller Mount, Weller Place, Weller Terrace, Weller Road, Weller View. Sometimes he would bring his children in, Nellie Grove, Back Nellie Grove, Archie Street, Archie Place, Doris Crescent, Back Doris Crescent, or use long words—Stipendiary Street, Industrial Street, Back Cemetery Lane. But the houses would be much the same, just as crowded only a little more or less pretentious according to their dates, and always among them, like the house of God, black mills and blacker chapels and churches.

SALFORD in the hard years of unemployment and the dole slouched and shivered among the identical houses of yesterday, its streets in winter enveloped in a greasy and acrid twilight. Here between the nude, black patches of land called 'crofts', waterlogged, sterile, bleak and chill, jungles of tiny houses were cramped and huddled together, the cradles of generations of the future. 'Places', wrote Walter Greenwood, 'where men and women are born, live, love and die and pay preposterous rents for the privilege of calling the grimy houses "home".'

A threepenny bus ride out of LEEDS city square, a train journey over the viaduct into WAKEFIELD or a coach trip to LIVERPOOL will show how slowly change comes to these Victorian enclaves in the land of 'Labor Omnia Vincit'.

BARNSLEY, to George Orwell's amazement a generation ago, built a new £150,000 Town Hall whilst still needing 7,000 working class houses and possessing only nineteen men's slipper-baths for a total population of 70,000. A recent critic, travelling round the big industrial cities of the North could not 'help but feel that this is simply not a tolerable way for people to be made to live in the mid-twentieth century. No amount of washing machines or TV sets could compensate for such squalor (*Encounter*, 1963.)

Festival Flats and Coronation Cottages began to spring up in JARROW at the end of the Second World War when some urgency

was put into the drive to replace sub-standard dwellings.[1] The
houses near the centre were for active working families and the
cottages, with common rooms, on an estate for old people. Clearance is planned of all insanitary and unfit houses until people can
have homes of up-to-date amenity and appearance. There will
soon be multi-storey flats in the Market Square area. Jarrow, 'the
town that was murdered', has found in these and the trading
estates a fresh will to live.

The tale of Quarry Hill Flats erected near the centre of LEEDS
in the shape of a colossal housing fortress on a clearance site
differs: they soon began to turn into another near slum. A better
solution perhaps may be found in the prefabs widely spreading
over the outlying suburbs and in the local authority 'rehabilita-
tions'. At WORKINGTON, Cumberland, where slum clearance has
led to the Council erecting nearly 3,000 houses since the last war,
'Regimentation of pattern has been mitigated through the use of
prefabricated methods, embodying modern features of equipment
and design with traditional modes of construction. Industrial
development and housing have been treated as one entity. The
houses, within easy reach of the new factories, have been laid
out with gardens and grass verges, and are *purely residential in
character*' (*Official Guide*: my italics). In short anything rather
than building barracks for the workers again, or the 'monumen-
tal tenements run mad' which create visual bedlam in the whole
fabric of areas like PRESTON.

Just before the Second World War a quarter of England's
urban population was living in houses with less than the minimum
statutory space allowance. Cities such as LEEDS, LIVERPOOL, NEW-
CASTLE, SHEFFIELD had many thousands of homes of a type
universally condemned. Since the war great strides have been
taken towards paying off the long debt owed to workers of a
decent place to live though MANCHESTER with 68,000 slum cottages on its conscience only managed to demolish 9,000 in seven

[1] Standards vary: but the five amenities for which Government grant
becomes available to an 'improving' landlord consist of bath, wash-hand
basin, hot water supply at three points, WC in or near to the house and a
ventilated food cupboard.

Landscape: Pennine barriers

49

Landscape: Heights above Huddersfield

Landscape: Old Macclesfield

Landscape: Burslem centre

Landscape: (above) Stoke outskirts; (below) In Calder valley

Landscape: (left) From Wear Bridge; (below) Approach to Wigan

Home: (above) Back-to-backs, Wigan; (below) New flats, Wigan

Home: Wash-day, Workington

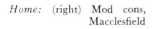

Home: (right) Mod cons, Macclesfield

(left) Easington, Co Durham

57

Home: Peterlee

Home: (above) Old Sheffield. . . ; (below) and new

Home: Model Place, Darlington

Work: (left) Hand-
weaving

(below) Spinner, Workers
Yorkshire Costumes,
Leeds 1814

Work: Regency silk mill

Work: Early cotton mill

Work: (above) Reducing and roving, yesterday; (below) Weaving today

years: another 700 collapse annually! Some comfortably-off critics have talked of pampering the working classes. The story has gone the rounds repeatedly of families moved into new houses who all huddled into one room and put the coals in the bath. Much has been made of isolated examples such as the new town PETERLEE,[1] built on a hilltop in the 50s to house 30,000 miners from decayed Durham villages around, and after fifteen years holding only 14,000 people. In spite of there being 'houses very close together so that miners can keep their tightly knit community life' the majority stayed in or returned to the slag heaps and grimy compression of places like SHOTTON with their clustering pubs, working-men's clubs and rickety cottages. Less has been said of the houses from which some families have come—with holes in the floorboards, cellars boarded up, bedrooms too damp to use, sulphur candles needed regularly to keep down bugs and lice.

SHEFFIELD—one of the first cities to prohibit the further building of back-to-back houses (1864)—has made housing its chief objective in city planning: using the ridges and hillocks of the old slum area it has devised in the Park Hill street-decks a means of neighbourly living comparable with the old terrace streets on the ground, cliffs of houses not jammed in among industrial sprawl but integrated with the landscape.

(Sheffield aims to live down Ruskin's tag 'a dark picture in a golden frame'. At present about two-thirds of the city is covered by smokeless zones. Sheffield Corporation's smoke-control department has launched a campaign to clamp down on 'nondescript' coalmen who are thwarting the attempt at making the city completely smokeless by selling coal in the zones where it is prohibited.)

Comparative figures, published January 1963 by the Association of Health Inspectors, in the slum-clearance drive:

	Unfit houses in 1955	Now cleared
LEEDS	22,500	11,900
BIRMINGHAM	50,200	˙ 10,300

[1] One of five being built in the NE—Newton Aycliffe, Washington, Cramlingham and Killingworth being the others.

MANCHESTER	68,000	9,500
LIVERPOOL	88,000	7,700
SHEFFIELD	13,500	6,000
BRADFORD	11,148	5,768

৩৵৵৩

As the whole transition from country to town in the 1800s led to troublous conditions, so the wholesale uprooting of the so-called slum population, even if it is transplanted into airier suburbs, can be expected to bring difficulties today. The unfamiliar neighbourhood, shops, pubs, domestic oven, journey to work, require a period of acclimatisation. But in the words of a house-wife, recently moved out of a slum into a new estate: 'When we first came here a lot of them thought it was too quiet, but I said: "I'm going to dig a hole in the garden and sit there until I take root." ' A garden for the first time is a fine thing to those trying to recover the taste of a forgotten heritage.

Some near-slum streets in BRADFORD have meanwhile been given a new lease of life by Pakistani immigrants and, on the outside at least, transformed by their décor of bright red, yellow, orange, white, olive, blue, green or turquoise paint, whatever their over-crowded or insanitary condition.

Inside, change and better times (generally) have affected the appearance but not the spirit of the home. The aspidistra, set in the window between half-length curtains, has given place to the colourful plaster figure of 'country-lad-eating-cherries' type, or more likely a shapely negress or a single, lifelike Alsatian. Instead of old-fashioned mahogany there is now veneered or varnish-stained chain-store furniture; chrome, cheap lustre and plastic knicknacks fill mantelpiece and sideboard instead of lacquered tea-caddy, moustache cup and shell-decorated photo frames; and instead of the window-box with bright geraniums or nasturtiums there are roses or begonias or gloxinias also made of plastic. The rag or 'clip' rug, of black or navy blue with a central diamond or circle perhaps in red, has been replaced by a jazz-patterned article of half the wearing quality. There may be leaded and tinted window panes. But the total effect remains as before: colour to offset

drab surroundings, a bit of show for pride's sake and the neighbours—not unlike the whitening or yellowing of sills and steps—
and the crowded, cluttered warmth of a family living room. Home
means sanctuary from the harsh world outside—even if washing
has to be strung across it and the street door opens almost on to
the tea-table.

WORK

There is undoubtedly a pleasure in reading recitals of horrible injustice and tyranny.

Diary, Arnold Bennett, 1918
(re Hammonds' Town Labourer)

I am noted for being able to keep the children awake and going longer than any other man in the mill.

Life and Adventures of a Factory Boy,
Frances Trollope, 1840

Industry and prudence conquer.

Accrington Town Motto

The early Victorian employer worked like a slave—and ruled like a slavemaster. In the changeover from the old system, where trades such as wool-combing, weaving, nail-making, cutlery depended solely on handskill and in which the workman's cottage could be both home and workshop, to the machine-fed factory system of operatives subjected to mill routine, the remedy for discontent was believed to be the incentive offered by work itself. Work offered to the labourer the prospect of ceasing to be a poor man : it offered him advancement by industry and merit without dependence on the patronage of squire or parson. He could become his own master and keeper of his own conscience while contributing to the richness and greatness of England. From the Industrial Revolution men peacefully obtained that freedom to make the most of themselves in competition with their fellows which the French revolutionaries had sought with bloody violence.

So when a self-made man exchanged his clogs for a coronet,

69

beholden to nobody, he then expatiated to others on the virtue of beginning at the bottom : the motto of the age was 'self-help'. Sir Robert Peel (2nd baronet), in opposing the workmen's Ten Hours Bill, said that he could name a dozen men who had risen from wages of twenty or twenty-five shillings a week to possessing fortunes over £100,000. *Vincit omnia perseverantia*;[1] and especially with the multiplication of labour's output-rate made possible by machinery.

The philosophy behind this attitude stemmed from Adam Smith. The Glasgow professor's tenet that the wealth of men and nations depended on the unimpeded operation of economic law, with the necessary hardships due to variations in supply and demand, and the theory that only by leaving every man free to pursue his own interest could production keep pace with the rise of consumption in an age of increasing population, bamboozled even champions of humane reform. Complete freedom of contract was the policy recognised both by manufacturers and administrators as the only means of maintaining the nation's producing power in the face of competition abroad. By it almost any inhumanity could be justified. As the world market was unpredictable, a 'reserve' of labour—or body of unemployed—was indispensable to tap as the man of capital required. What actually took place in the new factory towns of the North and Midlands, rough, remote and little visited before the railways linked up North and South (even then Dickens penetrated as far as PRESTON only once, while writing *Hard Times*) could not be expected to take legislators' attention from the far more pressing problems which England faced after a disastrous war with the American colonies and *vis-à-vis* revolutionary and Napoleonic France.

Enlightened manufacturers, of course, recognised that the change from cottage to mill would not be welcomed by their workers. In the first place switching from hand-loom to machine loom meant that fewer operatives were needed until market demand and output substantially increased. (Hand-loom cotton weavers had for a time benefited from steam-powered spinning

---

[1] Town motto of Whitehaven.

machinery : whereas formerly spinners could not give them enough yarn, in the 1790s so much was available that their employment was steady. Bolton weavers, receiving 3s 6d per yard for the fashionable fancy muslins, are said to have gone about the streets with five pound notes stuck in their hatbands. But as the labour market became flooded and machine weaving absorbed spinning output, wages soon fell.) The Luddite iron-loom-breakers who took matters into their own hands in the North and Midlands, 1811-12, made the situation worse for those seeking employment.

Then the conditions were oppressive : rising at five in the morning, called to work by the factory bell at six, working until six at night with only meal intervals, strict enforcement of discipline, with fines and sharp orders from the overlooker, the hot, close air and loss of nearly all personal liberty except on Sunday. All was very different from the irregular, undisciplined methods of the old industries, where bouts of hard work were followed by whole days off and journeymen in SHEFFIELD, frame knitters in NOTTINGHAM or ribbon weavers in COVENTRY who absented themselves from Saturday to Tuesday could put in excessive hours for the rest of the week to make up. Machinery could not be worked economically in that fashion.

To the evils from which the domestic worker had suffered the Industrial Revolution added discipline, and the discipline of a power driven by a competition that seemed as inhuman as the machines that thundered in factory and shed.

A spinner at Tyldesley, near MANCHESTER, who worked in a temperature of 80 to 84 degrees was subject to the following penalties :

Any spinner found with his window open	1s 0d
Any spinner found dirty at his work	1s 0d
Any spinner found washing himself	1s 0d
Any spinner leaving his oil can out of its place	1s 0d
Any spinner repairing his drum banding with his gas lighted	2s 0d

Any spinner slipping with his gas lighted	2s 0d
Any spinner putting his gas out too soon	1s 0d
Any spinner spinning with gaslight too long in the morning	2s 0d
Any spinner being five minutes after the last bell rings	1s 0d
Any spinner being sick and cannot find another spinner to give satisfaction must pay for steam per day	6s 0d
Any spinner found in another's wheelgate	1s 0d

At Tyldesley they worked fourteen hours per day, including the nominal hour for dinner; the door was locked in working hours, except half an hour at tea time; the workpeople were not allowed to send for water to drink, in the hot factory; even the rainwater was locked up, by the master's order, otherwise they would be happy to drink even that.

Part quoted from Political Register 1823 in The Town Labourer,
J. L. and Barbara Hammond, 1917

Workmen from the Lancashire and Yorkshire border expressed it more forcibly. 'Harry them o fro' their feythers' graves an' owd whoams. Bury them i' back entries i' th' teawns. Ring 'em to th' factory by strike o' day. Stifle 'em wi' stink, an' cotton fluff an' heat : drive 'em wi' overseers like slaves. When yo'n getten t'heart out on 'em, send 'em to a cellar to dee o' feyver, or consumption. Work mon an' wench together, an' ruin 'em body an' soul. Nowt but wark, driving, fining, bagging, harrying, worrying, fainting an' deeing.' From airy places like Pendle, Rossendale, Oswaldtwistle, spinners and weavers were forced to seek employment in the smother of MANCHESTER. The cotton trade was indeed the first to be radically affected by machinery, although the first English factory in the modern sense was John Lombe's silk-throwing mill, powered by water, in Derby on which Charles Roe's throwing factory in Macclesfield was modelled (1756). Up to 1830 the handskills were paramount in other textile work.

Cotton spinning must have been largely a factory industry by 1812, two-thirds of the trade being carried on by means of Crompton's mule which directly employed 70,000 people. (Crompton was shamefully deceived by those who agreed to pay him for publicly demonstrating his mule, though the spinning firms made fortunes by it.) By 1833 there were 85,000 power looms in England : there were still 250,000 handlooms in use, however, for fabrics which machines could not produce. For woollen manufactures only about 5,000 power looms were operating in 1835 and for another twenty years the majority of piece-working weavers in Yorkshire remained outside the factories.

Power looms for linen and silk weaving and the factory concentration of workers increased gradually from the mid '30's to the '50's.

A Hundred Years of Economic Development in Great Britain,
C. P. Jones and A. G. Pool, 1940

What was sauce for the gander, the employer whose one concern was to get riches and the exceptional workman, especially the mechanic or engineer, who might hope by industry to rise his equal, was—or had to be—sauce for the goose. A Lancashire cotton manufacturer in Regency times could hire 500 workmen one week and dismiss them the next, his responsibility for their welfare beginning and ending at the factory gate. He was concerned only with paying as little for, and getting as much out of, his labour as possible. If obsolescence of hereditary handskill or unemployment did not drive the workman to lower his wage demands, the manufacturer, enjoying complete freedom of contract, could always hire women or children or some half-starved Irish, of whom 100,000 had settled in Lancashire by 1835. Their wages were only a half or a third of the workman's and with 'strappers' to flog drowsy factory children awake, or hymn-singing to keep them so, production figures could be kept up. After all, when spinning or weaving machinery had been installed practically all that was left to be done by hand was the piecing together of broken threads, a task calling for nimble fingers rather than muscular strength. The more developed bones and muscles of the hands of grown men were actually unsuitable for this : they supervised frames of mule spindles helped by several 'piecers', youths or women. Girls and women alone worked the throstle spindles. To one MP a Scottish mill of this period 'seemed more to resemble a receptacle of demons than the workhouse of industrious human beings'.

Successive Reports on Children in Manufactories left no doubt about the 'horrible injustice and tyranny' inflicted both on women and children in this *laissez faire* factory system. One mill worked them from 5 am until 8 pm with only half an hour's respite for breakfast and dinner, six days a week and required part of their Sunday for cleaning the machinery. Pauper apprentices from urban slums, handed over by the Guardians to millowners, slept in shifts in barrack-like 'prentice houses and were kept almost continuously at work until either their age made their labour less profitable—or they died.

During the transition from cottage to factory work mothers and children were forced by want into accepting even these conditions. In 1839 about seventy per cent of the operatives in woollen, silk and flax mills were female, fifty per cent in cotton mills, and of 242,000 female factory employees, 112,000 were under the age of eighteen. For young girls guiding bobbins, winding cotton or making nails the hardship was not only physical. 'By constantly associating with depraved adults they fall into their ways—drink, swear, fight, smoke, sing and care for nobody.' Engels quoted a Manchester witness that three-quarters of girls between fourteen and twenty who worked in factories were 'unchaste' also. When such girls became in turn wives and mothers they might perhaps add a third to the household's weekly wages, but by their total ignorance and carelessness of household skills and duties probably wasted a half of the joint income. The child had had no time to learn needlecraft, neatness, cleanliness, economy : some could not so much as boil a potato. Again, in vicious sequence, such a wife working twelve or thirteen hours a day in the factory, had no chance to train *her* children. The home out of which they were thrust into the mill at five years old, to add a shilling to the week's earnings, was likely to be an untended hovel. (In a less aggravated form this problem still persists: unrestricted female employment and the incidence of juvenile delinquency seem more than coincidental.)

ᏳᏉᏉ

A committee to consider the state of children in manufactories, in 1816, took the evidence of forty-three witnesses—not one of them a worker. The group consisting of employers and employers' spokesmen, ridiculed the idea that the children were overworked. They admitted that the regular factory hours varied from thirteen to fifteen a day, that is from 6 am to 7 pm or from 5 am to 8 pm, but these hours they said agreed with the children wonderfully. Factory children were healthier, more intelligent, more moral than others: looks were deceptive: when long hours had to be worked the children were less tired than the adults. For the children's sake they deprecated shorter hours: it would be exceedingly prejudicial to their morals to let them out earlier. 'Nothing,' said one of these philanthropists who worked his children from 5 am to 8 pm, 'is more favourable to morals than habits of early subordination, industry and regularity.'

As for taking an hour or two from children's working hours that 'would amount to a surrender of all the profits of the establishment.'   The Town Labourer, J. L. and Barbara Hammond 1917

ᏨᎯᏗᎧ

'The factory population of Lancashire and the West Riding was discoloured and stunted and seemed more like some ill-fated race of pigmies than normal human beings' (Sir Arthur Bryant). Mothers obliged to remain at work until shortly before confinement and to return to the mill immediately after, children standing at a bench all day or working in crouched postures in hot, damp, crowded rooms—should it surprise that these 'racial' characteristics developed and sometimes can still be observed among third or fourth generation factory workers.

I can have no hesitation in stating my belief from what I saw myself that a large mass of deformity has been produced at BRADFORD by the factory system. The effect of long and continuous work upon the frame and limbs is not indicated by actual deformity alone: a more common indication of it is found in a stunted growth, relaxed muscles, and slender conformation.

This statement was made over a hundred years ago, in the first report of the Factories Enquiries Commission. The writer also has seen many a dwarfed, twisted, pigeon-chested figure in clogs and shawl or overalls among the crowds at 'losing' time in BRADFORD, KEIGHLEY, COLNE or BURNLEY. 'Stocky' or 'stiff-set' is the term they apply to themselves : 'stubby', 'bandy' or 'bowed' others call their short bodies and crooked legs.

Lord Macaulay allowed that a factory child might produce more in a single day by working twelve or fifteen hours instead of ten : he absolutely denied, however, that a great society in which children work fifteen or even twelve hours a day will, in the lifetime of a generation, produce as much as if those children had worked less. A contemporary of Macaulay, Anna Jameson, exposed the criminal folly of a social system 'that abounds with strange contradictions, in law, morals, government, religion : but the greatest, the most absurd, the most cruel of all is the banishment of woman from her home, in childhood, girlhood, wifehood' for the sake of labouring in factories.

Already, before these critics had raised their voices, before Disraeli had penned his black page on the mine, where 'on hands and feet an English girl, for twelve, sometimes sixteen, hours a day hauls and hurries tubs of coal up subterranean roads, dark, precipitous and plashy' the Condition-of-England question in the industrial areas had led evangelical reformers like Lord Ashley to press over and over again for government action. His proposed Bill for limiting the hours of children in textile mills to ten a day was obstructed as a measure that would seriously affect one-sixth of England's producing power. Philanthropy prevailed but slowly. Early factory reforms concentrated on the use of 'indentured' child labour in cotton mills with a view to prohibiting employment of children under nine and restricting the hours for those under sixteen to twelve per day. Determined manufacturers contrived to dodge the prohibitions. In 1833 it was secured that in *all* textile mills except those making lace no person under eighteen should be required to work in the night shift between 8.30 pm and 5.30 am or for more than twelve hours daily. Three years later for children under thirteen the maximum laid down was nine hours

and eventually, by the efforts of Ashley and others, a new Factory
Act (1843) limited the hours of children under sixteen to six and
a half, and also strengthened the regulations for inspection of industrial premises and fencing of machinery.

 ᕭᕥᕤ

In the novel *Sybil*, 1845, for which Disraeli spent some time
in the industrial north to acquire first hand material, one of the
most poignant scenes is the gathering of workmen's wives on
'Grand Tommy-Day'. As they try to select goods from the
employer's shop to be booked against their husband's wages,
various sharp practices are brought to light : short weight in
butter, top price for low-quality cheese, white-clay in flour,
things entered in her 'tommy-book' that a woman who could not
'figure' never had, imposition of orders of best tea or a whole
peck of flour or 'engine-room' bacon on complaining customers.
To Jones's wife, who brings a ticket for 3s 6d only out of
18s wages, the shopkeeper retorts : 'There's your money : and
you may tell your husband that he need not take his coat off
again to go down our shaft.'

A Truck Act of 1831, renewed in 1871, made it illegal to
force workmen to take payment in goods, but the law was
evaded. In Staffordshire 'butties' engaging miners on contract
themselves opened shops and by paying wages only once a
month forced workmen to buy from them on credit.

 ᕒᕤᕥ

Fines and the 'truck' system of paying wages in goods—corn
or cheap flour—were other running sores both in mill and mine.

The poor weavers who are perhaps only receiving 3s 6d or 4s
a week are constantly mulcted by these overlookers who have
their own wages paid out of what they can deduct from these
plundered wretches and a percentage on the amount. Then again
they have not even the small amount paid in money—it is paid
in goods—in rotten corn—in cheap flour, the quality being so
bad that he (the weaver) finds the flour which he had received
the previous week still unconsumed, the stomachs of his sickly
children had been unable to retain it (W. B. Ferrand, MP for
Bingley).

When as not infrequently happened, the goods were supplied
from a merchant who was also a publican and who took the line

that drink should first be bought out of the week's earnings or 'credit', precious little if anything was left to take home. The workman's world, where in the cotton-printing industry one man could now do with a machine and the assistance of one child the work done formerly by 200 block printers—turning out twenty-eight yards of printed cloth per minute—seemed in plain truth to be one

> Where fast and faster our iron master
> The thing we made, for ever drives,
> Bids us grind treasure and fashion pleasure
> For other hopes and other lives.

The 'feel' of mill conditions, in the period of ten years just before mid-century when exports of mixed wool and cotton fabrics from the West Riding alone were expanding from 2,400,000 to 42,115,000 yards annually and when imports of raw cotton into Lancashire were rising from about 200,000 to 350,000 tons, is vividly if fancifully portrayed in Dickens' 'Coketown':

> The streets were hot and dusty in the summer day. . . . Stokers emerged from low underground doorways into factory yards wiping their swarthy visages and contemplating coals. The whole town seemed to be frying in oil. There was a stifling smell of hot oil everywhere. The steam-engines shone with it, the dresses of the Hands were soiled with it, the mills throughout their many storeys oozed and trickled it. The atmosphere of those Fairy palaces was like the breath of the simoon : and their inhabitants, wasting with heat, toiled languidly in the desert. But no temperature made the melancholy mad elephants (pistons) more mad or more sane. Their wearisome heads went up and down at the same rate in hot weather and cold. For the summer hum of insects, it (Coketown) could offer, all the year round, from the dawn of Monday to the night of Saturday, the whirr of shafts and wheels.

Mechanical multiplication of productive processes offered un-exampled opportunities to anyone with capital : cheapening the price and vastly increasing the quantity of goods, was the sure way to world market dominance and fortune. But unequal division of the profits of trade between the head and the hand had never been so glaringly manifest. The principle of a fair wage to the workman willing to labour was forgotten. When fluctuations in trade led to price-cutting, wage-reductions and unemployment so that BURNLEY weavers could earn only 7½d a day and STAFFORD colliers had their daily rate lowered, while the price of corn was artificially kept up by the Corn Laws, then the slaves at last rebelled. Monster demonstrations in support of the People's Charter—the keystone of which was immediate transfer of electoral power from the middle, propertied class to the numerically superior labouring class—were followed by riots at STALYBRIDGE, OLDHAM, and MANCHESTER. Later that August of 1842 there came from STOCKPORT ('one of the darkest and smokiest holes in the whole industrial area': Engels) PRESTON, BURSLEM, then from almost every industrial town between LEICESTER and TYNESIDE, reports of furnaces extinguished, plugs hammered out of boilers and mills at a standstill. Bakeries, shops, town halls, police stations, railways were attacked. For almost a fortnight riot—the Plug Plot riot—held the day. It was not until regular troops and artillery were drafted into MANCHESTER and BOLTON was patrolled by Highlanders that violence and insurrection crumbled again into hunger and despair.

Results of the riots were not immediate, but the voice of reform began at last to be listened to above the claims of economic righteousness. Additionally the repeal of the Corn Laws, following on the Irish potato famine, eased the conflict. The Corn Laws, symbolic of the whole obsolete tariff structure, were most strongly opposed in Manchester. Not only did the growing population of the industrial North need regular food supplies at moderate prices—food which the British farmers were unable to supply in adequate quantity—but impoverished farmers of the corn-exporting regions of Europe, being prevented by British duty on imported corn from securing a regular market for their surplus, could not afford to buy British manufactured goods. After the repeal of the Corn Laws (1846) cotton exports to and grain imports from eastern Europe *both* appreciably mounted.

The Ten Hours Bill brought in during the slump year 1847 was an instrument of peace. It was not possible to organise mill work so as to combine a twelve hour day for adults with a ten hour day for those under eighteen, and so ten hours became law for workmen too. The reform was further strengthened by fixing meal times and the hours within which the working day must fall. In practice many northern millowners, like Salt of SALTAIRE and Marshall the linen manufacturer of LEEDS, were by then already working their men an eleven hour day. If not given his share of the profits of trade the workman now at least acquired his right to the larger life and his share in the leisure and culture open to other classes, instead of the soul-destroying formula of 'eating, drinking, working and sleeping'. Someone on the Short Time Central Committee had asked, what was the use of making public parks for those with no time to perambulate them or providing public baths for people who did not leave work till eight o'clock at night? Common sense and other pressures encouraged further reforms and the bringing of workshops into line with factories, while Forster's Education Act of 1870 which made elementary education compulsory was the next obvious step—to abolish illiteracy among the workers.

Out of the matrix of this first half of the Century of Commerce and for after generations out of the equally harsh pattern of the slump years between the wars, has been formed the temper of the Northern industrial worker and his attitude to employment and employer. Outsiders cannot know what the struggle to live means or 'what life is all about'. No one is more resistant to the 'plummily explanatory tone of the master-official', to 'fancy talk' or theory, to the idea of 'being taken in', than the workman in this world of work for bosses, where it is assumed that cash rules and everyone is out for gain, where he knows he will be discharged if that is the way of keeping the firm afloat. 'Y'never get owt for nowt', 'there's a catch in it somewhere', or (if something goes wrong) 'they'll see y' carry th' can alright' are his watchwords. There are pockets of industry, of course, where craftsmanship can still be enjoyed for its own sake, is properly paid and respected accordingly.

Certain firms have begun to make something of a fetish of 'good relations', their aim being 'to produce the finest goods under the most efficient, the most up-to-date and the healthiest and happiest conditions'. Or again, to quote its own publicity, 'Service, efficiency and happy faces' summaries one firm's ideal. (The ideal is not easy to impose on a system where every day the machine becomes more and more of a man, and the man more and more of a machine.)

Then the average workman's attitude to those who may have employed him and his people for generations will be a subtler mixture of familiarity, affection and resentment together with pride in their product. After all 'they've never done a real day's work in their lives'.

∽◇∼

There are two kinds of people in a mill : those who remember and those who don't. Those who remember—the Slump, that is; short-time and 'layings-off'; dole queues sprawling down grimy streets—still seem grateful to have a job at all.

To have been put-upon, victimised, pushed around and generally exploited is, for these people, almost a point of honour. Like battle veterans, comparing scars, spinners and weavers alike, strippers and grinders, carders and doffers will vie with one another as to who has taken most punishment.

Those who don't remember are altogether different. They take days off, eat in Chinese restaurants, go ten-pin bowling and on Continental coach tours : all of which, in the eyes of the older generation, comes dangerously close to tempting fate. Only in one thing do the two groups come together. An unwavering dislike for the management unites them, a common distrust of clean collars, polished shoes and aitches that aren't dropped.

Observer, 6 November 1966, Peter Kemp

∽◇∼

By Exhibition year, industrial England had turned the corner of the hungry and troubled 30s and 40s. Railways everywhere cheapened the cost of coal, provisions, clothes; gold discoveries in America and Australia led to increased demand for British goods and gold in payment; new capital and better transport opened fresh markets. In north Staffordshire, south Lancashire, the West Riding—the hub of the industrial wheel—trade began to boom, and as employment expanded, wages could go up and conditions be eased without loss to employers. Once the exacerbation of feelings caused by riot had diminished and the worst examples taken from the Reports of the Commissioners for Inquiring into the Employment of Children in Mines and Manu-

E

factories had been dealt with, the sympathies of visionaries and
moralists were directed towards other aspects of factory life.

> 'Twas August, and the fierce sun overhead
> Smote on the squalid streets of Bethnal Green,
> And the pale weaver through his window seen
> In Spitalfields look'd thrice dispirited.

While Arnold sonneteered on the South, pitying the preacher who
toiled there as much as the workman, Ruskin complained that
'as soon as one mill is at work, occupying two hundred hands, we
try, by means of it, to set another mill at work, occupying four
hundred. What is it to come to? How many mills do we want?'
Kingsley felt anxiety that 'mill labour effeminates the men and
makes them unfit for any other sort of labour—exclusively per-
forming day by day the same mechanical operation, till their
whole intellect is concentrated on it and their fingers kept delicate
for the purpose'. Precise answers to those worrying questions were
not given, but 'to soften the feelings of the working multitude' in
Disraeli's phrase and bridge the gulf between the two Englands
a new series of measures was brought in. Disraeli, perhaps more
clearly than any other public man, had heard the wail of intoler-
able serfage in the midst of the Utopia of wealth and toil that was
to be set up by breathless worshippers of Mammon.

Apart from the enforcement of safety regulations in factories,
inspection of industrial premises and allowance of a Saturday
half-holiday, which by this time were already on the statute book,
in 1875 the workman was placed on the same legal footing as his
employer in bargaining and trades unions were given the protection of the law. No trades union henceforth was illegal merely
because it was 'in restraint of trade' nor could it be sued or its
members imprisoned for the various actions customary in a strike,
such as 'watching and besetting' or 'picketing'. In the more
organised industries unions now gradually secured as wages a substantial share of the increased profits of trade. In negotiation with
employers they demanded a share in the direction of their members' labour—as well as regulations respecting overtime and piecework—and, to the fury of many old-style capitalists, used the

worker's vote to push Parliament into enforcing their demands
over the employer's head if necessary. The scope of Factory Acts
was steadily extended until the employer was made liable for all
the risks of his workers' employment and Labour Exchanges were
set up at the taxpayer's expense to find work for those unemployed
—instead of the old workhouses with their stigma of pauperdom
and combination of 'the maximum of deterrent with the minimum of subsistence'. A fair deal also was sought for the unskilled,
of whom there would always be a residue in a competitive world,
as for the skilled artisan who might emulate his master. Organised
labour was on the march to better the lot of its hands backed by
the experience gained in Chartism. The result could be called
the victory of the vanquished.

Impartial observers noticed a slackening in the industry of
operatives as early as the 80s: better hours, a living wage, union
protection were not everything.

> The great cry that rises from all our manufacturing cities,
> louder than their furnace blast, is all in very deed for this—that
> we manufacture everything there except men : we blanch cotton,
> and strengthen steel, and refine sugar, and shape pottery; but
> to brighten, to strengthen, to refine or to form a single living spirit,
> never enters into our estimates of advantages (Ruskin).

That was and still is the industrial dilemma : when combustion
power came in, true satisfaction in the job went out : factory
work deadened and dulled sensibilities, if it did not actually
brutalise. Day long, tending machinery demands their attention,
but exercises neither mind nor body. It might happen that in
SHEFFIELD or BIRMINGHAM the 'little mester' survived into the era
of the pneumatic hammer and machine press, working with three
or four men on file-cutting, knife-grinding, nail-making or gun-
assembling in his own small premises, but in most trades the
operative became just part of the machine. While abuses like that
of forty little girls licking labels by the mouth at the rate of thirty
gross a day until their tongues were polished at the tip and for
the rest coated with brown gum (Factory Inspectors' Report
1907), or 'half-timers' in the NOTTINGHAM lace trade ruining their
sight by the double work of school and factory, were winkled

out, the effects of further gearing up production by stereotyping
and sub-dividing of processes remained and are hardly less stulti-
fying. In 'dirty' trades, the brutalisation, the impact of crude
surroundings, constant din and coarse companions on young
apprentices, is no easier to disregard.

Extract from factory rules, early Victorian :

> IF any hand in the mill be seen
> TALKING to another, WHISTLING or
> SINGING he or she will be fined
> SIXPENCE   (quoted by Engels)

Sign hanging in machine shop : contemporary :

> WARNING TO GIRLS
> IF your SWEATER is too large for you
> Look out for the MACHINES
> IF YOU are too large for your sweater
> Look out for the MACHINISTS

The apprentice is 'fair game' to his seniors : sent to stores in
the foundry for a 'long stand' and kept waiting half an hour
while the storekeeper and the rest wink and snigger; set upon
after work, his trousers torn down and his exposed parts daubed
all over with dirty grease and red paint. Such is 'initiation'. 'Now
you'll be one of us: you've all got to go through it when you
first come.' (Sometimes mill girls used to expose raw lads this way
and called it 'sunning' them.) An engineering apprentice, in the
30s, though, was up against more serious tricks than this. He
would like to be a 'tradesman' with regular wages and a status
above that of the ordinary workman. After seven years in the
firm—'picking up' things in the workshop and jumping at the
infrequent chance to repair a lathe—with only fifteen shillings a
week, rising to thirty shillings at twenty-one on the pretext that he
is learning a trade, he finds that he never reaches the 'journey-
man' full-pay stage. As in most firms, the machinery is largely

automatic and doesn't need fully skilled men to run it. Some
machines, as for screw-making, can work twenty-four hours a
day without anyone going near them. So he 'gets his cards' while
the firm takes on a new batch of apprentices. Unless he wants
to spend the rest of his life on mass production jobs, the only
thing left is to go to technical school.

Crudity of working conditions, of course, was not confined to
the workshop or factory hand. Well into this century iron manufacture in Britain was a matter of brute force, not machine
process. Ironstone, lifted off trucks, fed into kilns, taken to and
drawn out of the furnace, loaded in 'pigs', was handled by men
amidst constant din, dust, danger to limbs and lungs, violent heat
or cold and heavy strain. The 'gantryman', feeding the kiln with
coal in the sulphurous fumes from the furnace, the 'charger' heav-
ing barrow-loads of ironstone, limestone and coke into the blast-
furnace, the 'scarrer' standing at the bottom of the kiln with a
heavy rod to break up fused masses for the hopper, the 'slagger'
struggling to control a glaring flood of molten metal when the
furnace was tapped, all endured a working world, black or flame-
coloured, either choked by gases or smothered in red, brown,
black or white deposits of dust.

The main direction of change in working life since the First
World War has been towards more and more comprehensive
organisation, mechanical aid, and large, impersonal manipula-
tion of employees. The result, in contrast to the rough, reckless
energy of nineteenth-century production, has been efficiency, but
with it increasing boredom. All the techniques of 'scientific management'—for highest possible output at lowest cost—have not
prevailed against it. The 'hand' has become an automaton : loss
of former industrial superiority based on cheap labour and coal
is made good by ever more 'mindless' tasks.

> Two hundred and fifty girls in the machine-room worked with
> the regularity of a blood-beat : a hand to the left, a hand to the
> right, the pressure of a foot : a damp box flew out, turned in
> the air and fell on the moving stair. It was impossible to hear the
> boxes falling, or a voice speaking, because of the noise of the
> machines.

Boredom claims its victims too :

A hand to the left, a hand to the right, the foot pressed down.
A finger sliced off so cleanly at the knuckle that it might never
have been, a foot crushed between revolving wheels.

Then, notes Graham Greene, the smooth procedure continues : sickness benefit, half wages, incapacity, the management
regrets . . . 'If there were no buttons to press nowadays they
would not know what to do with it,' said an old workman to the
present writer, with scornful pity.

༺∿∿༻

Arthur reached his capstan lathe and took off his jacket,
hanging it on a nearby nail so that he could keep an eye on
his belongings. . . . He smiled to himself and picked up a glit-
tering steel cylinder from the top box of a pile beside him, and
fixed it into the spindle. He jettisoned his cigarette into the
sud pan, drew back the capstan and swung the turret on to its
broadest drill. Two minutes passed while he contemplated the
precise position of tools and cylinder; finally he spat on to both
hands and rubbed them together, then switched on the sud-
tap from the movable brass pipe, pressed a button that set the
spindle running, and ran in the drill to a near chamfer.
At a piecework rate of 4s 6d a hundred you could make your
money if you knocked up fourteen hundred a day—possible
without grabbing too much and if you went all out for a
thousand in the morning you could dawdle through the afternoon and lark about with the women and talk to your mates
now and again. . . .
Though you couldn't grumble at four and six a hundred the
rate-checker sometimes came and watched you work, so that
if he saw you knock up a hundred in less than an hour Robboe
would come and tell you one fine morning that your rate had
been dropped by sixpence or a bob. So when you felt the
shadow of the rate-checker breathing down your neck you
knew what to do if you had any brains at all : make every
move more complicated, though not slow because that was
cutting your own throat, and do everything deliberately yet
with a crafty show of speed.

Saturday Night and Sunday Morning, Alan Sillitoe, 1958

༺∿∿༻

Industrial psychology, study of employee, machine and task as one unit, attempts to combine improved output with work-enjoyment. Welfare steps in where *laissez-faire* has been discredited. Instead of the 'strapper' there is incentive. In a mill at LEEK (motto *arte favente nil desperandum*), for example, 'departments are full of the noise of sewing machines and "Workers' Playtime", where girls with their hair in curlers and their machines draped with close-up shots of the pop-singers they dream about, stitch away at mountains of pink and yellow panties'. Overhead swing placards bearing their team names—Margaret, Alexandra, Anne, Marina. Competition is the thing—with bonus.

⟡

Less Fatigue, Higher Production—'fancy talk'

It has become part of the folklore of industry to attribute to fatigue variations in output as a work period proceeds. Allowance for this is usually built into the rate for the job. When work was heavy and physical, most people had a reasonable idea of what fatigue was—they got physically tired. But in modern industry relatively few people are now engaged in this kind of heavy work : far more often they are engaged in light work which can be both monotonous and boring. . . .

Research has been under way now for some time in an attempt to discover the nature of the changes that take place with time when work is light and monotonous. After shop floor investigations to define the problem, laboratory studies have been put in hand, under controlled conditions, in an attempt to discover factors which may influence changes in output as a work period proceeds. Phenomena have been observed which can be related to what might be described as the onset of 'mental fatigue'. Trials in which breaks were given at the point at which these phenomena occur have resulted in a higher and more regular performance than in those in which operatives were allowed to take rest when they felt so inclined : both being superior to working continuously.

Since we appear to be dealing with a mental phenomenon it might be expected that mild cerebral stimulants would have a beneficial effect. One such stimulus is caffein and a preliminary series of experiments has shown that when this is given in quantities equivalent to those contained in a 7 oz cup of coffee the improvement in output is higher than when a rest is taken alone or coffee taken without a rest.

Financial Times, April 1967

ᗺᏗᏗᎯ

The tacklers and tenters, doffers, winders and sidepiecers of LANCASHIRE factories—where to claim that one had been a four or possibly six-loom operative was a matter once for real pride— are now a diminishing race.[1] Textile production, for a generation undercut by foreign manufacture based on dirt cheap labour, is being streamlined into a system called 'verticalisation': with the most modern machines not one, but _all_ the processes of turning raw cotton into a print frock can be handled in the same organisation. The closure of 400 mills, 30 in BLACKBURN alone, since 1959 and a fall in the labour force of 42,000 in three years, tells its own tale. Where mills have not been demolished they are used for other purposes—as warehouses, mail-order centres, for production of electronic devices, plastics, until in Blackburn the majority of workers are now employed otherwise than in cotton. Spinners who have spent half a lifetime in cotton cannot find a spinning job any longer: young workers go off to acquire new skills. The situation in export trades makes dependence on one staple industry perhaps more precarious than ever before both for the manufacturer and for the community.

The wool sorter whose pace and skill in separating by touch rather than sight the qualities of greyish-yellow, greasy fleeces which to the uninitiated seem all alike has a knowledge and value indispensable in the wool trade. But if his skill were linked to one type of end product only and the economy of a town were linked exclusively with that product, his and the community's future would be an uninsurable risk today. In the nineteenth century the woollen industry at BATLEY (floreat industria) was the most important local undertaking, especially the mungo and shoddy trade which originated there, and in that period the

---

[1] They may soon have new names in an attempt to modernise: doffer = 'spinning assistant': stripper and grinder = 'card attendant': bobbin carrier = 'frame assistant': dirt-hole labourer = 'service operator'.

town's population increased tenfold. Batley still abounds in woollen-cloth manufacturers, woollen, cotton and yarn spinners, makers of blankets, carpets, felt, flock rugs, shoddy and mungo and in the linked trades of dyers, fullers, hair merchants, rag merchants and rag carbonisers, but recently the total pattern of industry has been transformed by the introduction of a dozen other traditional or contemporary industries. The whole economic life of the borough has gained a better balance with the availability of many more trades and types of labour. Such towns hitherto, relying upon one or two original sorts of employment, were all too dependent for their growth and economic stability on the prosperity of the basic local undertaking, and all too vulnerable.

That, of course, does not imply that this and other 'BATLEYS' are not keeping abreast of the times in their own special line. A mill founded there in 1845 for instance made industrial history in 1960 as the first woollen concern to instal the revolutionary four-colour Sulzer weaving machine from Switzerland: it has also recently perfected a special high-quality cloth with a 'rain-and-stain' finish.

Northern enterprise is a byword. Without it both master and man would have come far worse than they have out of the Century of Commerce. The extreme example of what could happen to a virtually one-industry town was provided by JARROW *(labore et scientia)* in 1934. Then a great shipyard, with its ancillary furnaces, rolling mills, boiler and engine shops, generator stations and joiners' shops, was 'bought out', with a covenant against ship-building in it for the next forty years. Three-quarters of JARROW's working population were immediately OUT also: the the town rotted and the time came when over two hundred men would apply for one vacancy as road-sweeper. The lesson of 'industrial diversification' was learnt, but only after prolonged hardship and heart-break. WORKINGTON, West Cumberland, dependent hitherto on coal, iron, steel and ship-building, after depression that reduced thirty-one per cent of its population to the dole queue, was eventually to seek similar cure. Its range of new industries, including those at neighbouring MARYPORT (over two-thirds of the population workless in the 30s) and WHITEHAVEN, now extends from the weaving of wool, rayon and silk, carpet and furniture manufacture to plastics, engineering components and chemical plants, not to mention the ramifications of nuclear fission.[1]

The roots of the past are strong but men cannot live on past or passing industrial conditions. Metamorphosis involves pride and in the North especially, pride is painful. In most mill towns, however, although the old names of the mills may remain on their totem chimneys—Waterloo, Wellington, Nelson, Trafalgar, Albion, Premier, Mons, or like ships, the Gresham, the Pilot, the Malta, the Egyptian—the battleground has changed. It is no longer *labor* alone, but *labor et varietas omnia vincunt*. There's bound to be 'a catch in it somewhere' they'll say, but 'It's a living, i'n't it?'

---

[1] Out of a labour force of 17,631, steel now employs 3,500 workers; out of five collieries working in 1960 two remain active: Workington still 'smells of depression'.

PLAY

---

*One Englishman a fool: two Englishmen a football match:
three Englishmen the British Empire.*

*The sterner sense of the Populace likes bawling, hustling and
smashing: the lighter self, beer.*

Culture and Anarchy, Matthew Arnold, 1869

The characteristic that led a wit to coin his epigram about the
English way abroad—'two Englishmen a football match'—is as
deeply rooted as any element in the national make-up. Football
first earned printed mention as a sport in the year 1175 and was
played throughout the Middle Ages in village rough and tumbles,
commonly on Shrove Tuesday—a habit still kept up in parts of
Derbyshire. It gave a healthy outlet for animal spirits and did the
village commons good, incidentally, by aerating the turf for new
spring grass.

Towards the end of the eighteenth century football playing
was on the wane and from 1820 to 1840 almost ceased. Why?
The chief reasons appear to have been that very many of the
former village lads were now townsmen, in the massive switchover
from agricultural to industrial employment: and with no Saturday half day the only chance for the working class to play was on
Sunday, when Lord's Day Observance Societies saw to it that
they didn't. An even more obstructive factor was that under the
Enclosure Acts commons and open spaces were fast disappearing;
in the chaotically built industrial towns they were practically
non-existent. . . . BOLTON with its 45,000 inhabitants had no public

91

open spaces: BLACKBURN had no place suitable for children's exercise or games: MANCHESTER's labouring population had no season of recreation and no amusements, except the theatre for the very few who went. In BIRMINGHAM there were originally gardens for working men, at about a guinea a year rent, where their families could go and spend evenings or Sundays in the little huts and summer-houses. Within a decade nearly all these gardens had been built over.

This loss of playgrounds, serious enough to call for a select committee to enquire into the deficiency of 'Public Walks and Places of Exercise', led after six years' agitation to the introduction of a Standing Order into Enclosure Bills (1844). Its provision was that 'an open space should be left sufficient for the exercise and recreation of the neighbouring population', when wastes and commons were enclosed. The interpretation was frequently farcical. BRADFORD had then a population of over 100,000 : when the 170 acres of FAIRWEATHER GREEN were enclosed 3 acres were reserved for people to play cricket and the local 'spell and knur' in which a ball would be driven ten or twelve score yards. Many a village in earlier times could have done better for a population of 100. When, as a consequence, children spun their tops or flew their kites and youths tried to run foot races in the streets and roads, such towns passed local by-laws and levied fines to quell the nuisance.

So, for the rapidly increasing populations, lodged in their narrow courts and confined streets of those towns engaged in the three great manufactures of the kingdom, cotton, woollens and hardware, the means of exercise in the fresh air and recreation or amusement with their families lessened every day. The fact that in the past all the world were in the habit of walking about on commons did not mean that they had acquired any right in law to do so. Even old paths were lost under the Enclosure Act which empowered commissioners to refashion the whole highway system. So cricket playing or football games became tantamount to trespass, whether in SHEFFIELD or BOLTON, OLDHAM or GATES-HEAD, perhaps not all at once but by gradual erosion of public spaces. At BASFORD, a framework-knitting town near NOTTING-

HAM, 1,200 acres of forest, common and waste were swept into private hands without one acre being left for public use.

∽◦◦∾

Football's survival was largely due to the public schools. Its resurgence began in the 1850's with the founding and influence of the Sheffield and Hallam clubs (the famous 'Wanderers') and the Blackheath Rugby Club. Then in the '60's and '70's came the F.A., the England Cup and Rugby Union. Northern Union or Rugby League, a professionals' game popular in Lancashire and Yorkshire, dates from 1893. In cricket the I Zingari was first in the field, 1845, and a regular all-England XI began to play a few years later.

∾◦◦∽

Games being virtually excluded from the working man's week what were the alternative distractions and recreations? Obviously man, 'the machine of machines', the machine compared with which all the contrivances of Watts and Arkwrights are worthless, needed time for repairing and winding up. Macaulay's appeal to the House, however, for proper weekend leisure for factory workers was not inspired by the wish to see them at play, but at family prayers, at church or at chapel. It was made as difficult as possible for this 'machine of machines' to exchange the discipline of the week in the factory for anything else than the discipline of Sabbath observances. Sunday spelled no work, but it also spelled no travel, no parks, no museums, no music, no playing in the streets, nothing but drabness for those who lived in tiny tenements. 'The aspect in the streets is that of an immense and well ordered cemetery' was one Frenchman's impression of an English Sunday—and quite feasibly the Sabbatarians' ideal.

William Hewitt, in a contribution to the *Literary Souvenir*, 1836, was moved to plead that mechanics 'caged by their imperious necessities in shops and factories during the week' and toiling 'amid the whirl of machinery and greedy cravings of mercantile gain' should not be cooped up by the bigots on Sundays also and caused 'to walk with demure steps and downcast eyes'.

He wanted them to be able to leave the great manufacturing towns to enjoy Sunday outings in the country, with freedom to 'walk in the face of heaven and the beauty of earth' as a change from their work-a-day dungeons.

Efforts were made by other well-meaning sympathisers to open some avenues of enjoyment to the working man on his day off. Their success was mimimal; in MANCHESTER and SALFORD the proposal, in the year of the Great Exhibition, to have Sunday bands in the parks was repulsed by the powers of Exeter Hall. In LIVERPOOL, all public walks, cemeteries (sic) and zoological and botanical gardens where the public might amuse themselves innocently were CLOSED ON SUNDAY. When it was suggested that the botanical gardens in LEEDS might be opened on Sundays for the benefit of the working classes, the idea was attacked as 'a wretched exchange to draw the poor out of their Churches, Chapels, Sunday Schools and quiet homes on the Lord's Day'. MANCHESTER'S zoological gardens on Sundays were firmly shut.

From John Wesley's early days the influence of the Methodists had been brought to bear against theatres—in NOTTINGHAM, HULL, MANCHESTER—as being 'peculiarly hurtful to [a] trading city, giving a wrong turn to youth especially, gay, trifling and directly opposite to the spirit of industry and close application to business'. They were now as active in denying recreation for mind or body in music or games, beauty of art or nature on the urban Sunday. Wherever Methodism spread among the employing class the population of the industrial towns suffered the consequences of the sect's reputation for saying 'No'. Not only did this Sabbatarian prejudice prevent free admissions to public gardens after morning service: Methodists prohibited organs and anthems in chapels, from fear of differentials or dilution in 'a form of service especially suitable for poor people', ie whole congregations singing.

Two of the Methodists' loudest 'noes' were directed at drink and gambling. But the rigid discipline within the fold caused many to spend their Sundays outside it, and at this period the Yorkshire and Lancashire papers were full of complaints about

town youths spending their Sunday playing pitch-and-toss at
street corners or in drunkenness and dog-fighting.

※

In SHEFFIELD on Sundays young people stand about the
streets all day gambling by tossing coins or by organising dog-
fights. They frequent gin-shops assiduously. In one low bar
visited (by the Commissioner, Children's Employment Commission 1842) forty to fifty young people of both sexes were
sitting. Nearly all of them were under seventeen years of age
and every youth had his girl friend with him. . . . In several
of the beershops, the young people were playing cards, while
in others they were dancing. But in all of them drinking was
going on. Known prostitutes were among the company. It is not
surprising to hear that in SHEFFIELD it is very common for
irregular sexual intercourse to take place at an early age and
that girls as young as fourteen or fifteen have already become
prostitutes. . . . It is difficult to decide which town should be
awarded the prize for the grossest immorality.

The Condition of the Working Class in England, Engels

At this time Manchester, with a population of 400,000, had 475
public houses and 1,143 beer houses.

※

If a clergyman was roused to complain that many services were
'blank, dismal, oppressive and dreary', it will scarcely surprise
that the lower classes, who had to toil wearily through every other
day, found Sunday the weariest of all. There was one door, however, that the 'Noes' failed to shut. When an evangelical peer
brought in a Bill (1856) for closing public houses on the Lord's
Day, the church parade of high society in Hyde Park was pelted
and abused on three successive Sundays, until the Bill was withdrawn. Kill-joy Sabbatarianism in fact helped to lead the populace into seeking solace where the folding doors opened to any
man who pushed his foot against them—the beershop and gin
palace. Bawling, hustling and beer were the working class reaction
to the frugal virtues of the new urban Sabbath.

There are days when you get up and go through th' hours just
longing for a bit of a change—a bit of a fillip, as it were. Men

have it stronger in 'em to get tired o' sameness and work for ever. And what is 'em to do? It's little blame to them if they do go into th' gin shop for to make their blood flow quicker and more lively and see things they never see at no other time—pictures and looking-glass and such like.

Gin at twopence a nip, or even less—'Drunk for 1d: Dead drunk for 2d: clean straw free' was a gin shop advertisement—was not the only solace of the workman whatever its notoriety. His taste had once been country-formed and a flower garden was still its expression when chance offered, the last 'art' of the slums. Well-meaning clerics like Dean Hole (founder of the National Rose Show, 1858) tried to encourage the artisan-florist in industrial areas. 'From flowers may be learned the road to the inner heart of the lower classes, the key to tastes dearer to them than beer-swilling, the secret which, if rightly applied by those who bear spiritual rule over the working man, may do much to civilise and indirectly to Christianise him.'

With or without such patronage, NOTTINGHAM stockingers, twist hands, shoemakers, tailors and mechanics would deny themselves rest to raise their favourite blooms. In tiny backyards and Lilliputian glasshouses they got results by taking in bags of coal throughout the winter before going to work, by using the blankets from their beds during a heavy frost, and by applying such compost mixtures as goose dung, sugar-baker's scum, night soil and yellow loam. Different towns specialised in different flowers: MACCLESFIELD in gold-laced polyanthus, DERBY in ranunculus, Middleton, LANCASHIRE and some YORKSHIRE florists in 'edged' auricula, PAISLEY in pinks and so on. Many flowers attracted the working man into shows and competitions—usually held in rooms hired from the 'Oddfellows', 'Foresters' or 'Druids'. Among them were the Christmas rose, chrysanthemum, crocus, tulip, pansy, dahlia and florist's rose and, in a class of it own, the giant gooseberry. For prizes there would be a copper kettle or brass pan. By the mid 40s auricula societies flourished in nearly every parish of northern England, there being several hundred distinct varieties with names such as Lancashire Hero, Grime's Privateer, Cockup's Eclipse, Lee's Venus, Flora's Flag—and many of the finest varieties were bred by weavers and miners. Some sturdy few are extant today and can be seen in the Northern Auricula Society's annual show held at Hangingditch, MANCHESTER. The 'Roaring Lions', 'Thumpers', and 'Crown Bobs' of the giant gooseberries, prizewinners all, were rivalled by giant leeks as specialities of artisan enthusiasm. In BLYTH, Northumberland, nearly every pub and club still runs a leek show : there are large cash prizes for leeks up to 12 in round and for nights before show day special guards are mounted against 'slashers'.

The allotment garden was the obvious answer to restrictions on the rational enjoyment of leisure inflicted on northern workers. Parts of the Midlands had a Labourers' Friendly Society with sixty-three branches which paid a joint amount direct to land-owners for the use of allotments, so skirting round the difficulty of collecting small rents from a large number of tenants. Few northern districts could supply the demand for such allotments. The excuses were that land near to towns was too valuable : the more that was given over to allotments, the less there would be for dividing up among the proprietors. A similar embargo on con-verting common and waste land prevailed in the 'Hungry Forties', when it was believed that high farming with artificial manures might turn Derbyshire hills and Yorkshire moors into prairies of waving corn. So enclosures were speeded up, while allotment provision stayed as before—meagre. As for other access, it was a further twenty years before the Commons Preservation Society began to arouse public support.

As with the working man's conditions, sympathy and attempts to improve his small degree of leisure first came from private and individual effort. Some millowners provided playgrounds, some gave libraries for their workpeople. Mechanics Institutions, orig-inated in the 20s by Dr Birkbeck and Lord Brougham to popu-larise scientific knowledge and to make the workman better at his work, also had their libraries and by mid-century some 100,000 members. A campaign for public free libraries and museums was started. Although Sunday opening of museums was out, eventu-ally an Act was passed (1850) to enable town councils to establish libraries, provided that two-thirds of the ratepayers consented to

F

the extra halfpenny rate. An energetic MP spent five years campaigning for the establishment of public walks, playgrounds, baths and 'places of healthy recreation and amusement'. A private owner gave to the town of DERBY its 'arboretum', which produced improvement both in the appearance and demeanour of the working people and probably in their health also. Eventually local authorities obtained use of the rates for parks as well, though as late as 1844 PRESTON was the only town in Lancashire with a public park. In LIVERPOOL the experiment was tried of giving good concerts at a price deliberately fixed to attract the working class and large attendances followed.

༄

MANCHESTER opened the first public library in 1852 : BOLTON, LIVERPOOL, SHEFFIELD, PRESTON soon followed suit. In 1843 BIRKENHEAD set aside 70 acres for recreation : in that decade MANCHESTER by private subscription and public grant bought three parks. BLACKBURN, HALIFAX, ROCHDALE, STOCKPORT obtained parks in the '50's and LEEDS bought Woodhouse Moor.

Progress report. PARKS, CEMETERIES and ALLOTMENTS.

Under this characteristic heading the current official handbook for HUDDERSFIELD (pop. 131,840) lists six parks, the first one opened in 1884 : two sets of playing fields, one still in preparation : three thousand allotments : a number of small ornamental gardens about the squares : three cemeteries and 'one of the best crematoria in the West Riding'. The parks total about 96 acres, the playing fields will have 64 acres and the crematorium stands in 14 acres of laid-out land. In addition there are numerous recreation grounds, varying in size from $\frac{1}{2}$ acre to 8 acres, with playground equipment or football pitches. The area of the borough as a whole is 14,149 acres.

༄

The next thing was to obtain time for the enjoyment of such amenities. Here MANCHESTER led the way : in 1844 the merchants granted a Saturday half holiday for all their employees. What use were the parks, baths, libraries if every manufacturing operative above the age of thirteen had a daily twelve hours' labour and up to fifteen hours' occupation? For him the most important event of all was the winning of the Ten Hours Bill in 1847, when play actually became a possibility in his life.

Another means of relaxation from the discipline of work, which flourished in many northern towns and which had been encouraged by law since the end of the eighteenth century, was the Friendly Society. Its primary aim was to help thrift and insurance, to act as sick and burial club, but the Friendly Society also provided social entertainment, gave workmen a taste of ceremony and pageantry, and helped to mould decent customs and manners. The present writer recalls his introduction into the Independent Order of Oddfellows in the smoke-filled upper room of a lodge just off a busy main street, as an occasion of dignified entry into a warm fellowship. For those used to taking orders membership of a society gave opportunity to take decisions also, and accept responsibility in the various roles of office. The range, from Temperance Society to Knight Templars and Loyal Ancient Shepherds and Shepherdesses to Royal and Antediluvian Order of Buffaloes, was wide enough to provide congenial activity for most temperaments. For long the Friendly Society or the club remained the exclusive bastion of the working man, but his womenfolk gradually penetrated it by infiltration. If one does not know which is club night in a northern town, one can soon guess nowadays from the sea of 'rollers' ('A flat head, glistening with metal curling-pins kept in all day'—Lady Bell, 1907) flowing out of the mills after work. (Some pubs, however still refuse women entry into their bars, just as some eating houses in Bradford and Halifax cater only for men.)

Equally strong in appeal but to traits other than thrift, self-improvement and self-esteem were the music halls. In the days when the only door open to the working man at the week's end was that of the public house, they started with songs and drink in the bar parlour on the do-it-yourself level of entertainment and led on to 'Harmonic Meetings', 'Free and Easies' and 'Catch and Glee Clubs'. Popular hostelries soon needed to convert rooms into regular halls where favourite performers appeared as well as local talent under a rumbustious chairman. The respectable classes stayed away, but up to the end of the century the working class

was held in the grip of the music hall as it is by TV today. The
Era Almanack for 1868 lists 300 halls outside London, among
them eight each in LEEDS and MANCHESTER, nine in BIRMINGHAM
and ten in SHEFFIELD.

 ᏳᏯᏳ

Pubs' Long Reign

The need for some provision for men's leisure is especially
conspicuous on a Sunday. Sunday is the workman's day of
leisure and he wants a place to go to that day where he will
be amused. An investigation recently made by a local temperance society (in Middlesbrough population nearly 97,000)
into the numbers who entered the public houses in the
town on a given Sunday, gave the following result. Into 106
public houses and 36 off-licences observed that day there
entered :   Men   55,045
             Women   21,594
             Children   13,775
                          ———————
          total of   90,414 persons.

The majority of these people probably belonged to the iron-
workers. As stated earlier there are 70,000 people who do not
go to church, a large majority of these belonging to the working classes, and of these, again, probably a considerable number
would like to find something attractive to do on this day of
leisure outside their homes. The workmen's clubs are not open
on Sunday, the theatres and music-halls are not open on that
day, nor is the Free Library, nor the museum. The public-
houses are open and are therefore frequented by the numbers
shown.   At the Works, Lady Bell, 1907

 ᏳᏯᏳ

(On weekdays, in some of the lower quarters, touts were employed
by the publicans, being given a free drink if they brought in a
customer, and standing on the pavement to ply the workman with
offers of drink, especially on pay-day.)

Some of the names of the songs of northern performers from
that half century are remembered yet. Harry Liston from the
60s with 'When Johnny comes marching home'; George Ley-
bourne, a former engine fitter, for 'Champagne Charlie' and 'The
Flying Trapeze' :

He taught her gymnastics and dressed her in tights
To help him live at his ease,
And made her assume a masculine name,
And now she goes on the trapeze.

'The Calico Printer's Clerk', sung by Harry Clifton: 'In MAN-
CHESTER that city of Cotton, Twist, etc.' Vesta Tilley first
appeared in NOTTINGHAM at the St George's Hall where her father
was 'chairman'. Tom Foy, 'The Yorkshire Lad', relied on his
northcountry humour: Jack Pleasants, a later Yorkshire
comedian, sang 'Twenty-one today', and 'I'm shy, Mary Ellen,
I'm shy' (he was) and 'Watching the trains go by'. The writer has
boyhood memories of Florrie Ford at Blackpool, G. H. Elliott
'The Chocolate-coloured Coon', and Bransby Williams, who used
to double his impersonation acts with monologues such as 'Enoch
Arden' given at Wesleyan chapels. George Formby (senior) 'The
Lad from Wigan' and Charles Whittle (of Bradford, who dressed
like a typical working man) with 'The Girl in Clogs and Shawl'
were the precursors of music-hall artistes whose origins in or
material from the industrial North have continued out of last
century into this: Gracie Fields of Rochdale, Sandy Powell ('Can
you hear me, mother?'), Jimmy Jewel whose father was a Yorkshire comedian. If the Southerner wanted to know what Glasgow
or Belfast, LEEDS, HULL or MANCHESTER were really like he need
only go to the music-hall variety to find out. There were all the
local jokes and sayings, there was the regional talent often later
to become famous throughout the country.

After the bioscope, Bijou or Palais de Luxe moving-picture
shows came into vogue, soon followed by palatial cinemas,
'talkies', rag-time, road shows and wireless, and music hall went
out. Films had a great appeal to the cotton operative and weaver,
offering two or three hours of dream-indulgence in all the luxury,
romance and adventure that their lives lacked. Many, in the 20s
and 30s, at the expense of their stomachs chose the pictures in
preference to the 'flea pit' (local theatre) and bought the cheapest
food to make do. 'Live for today and never mind tomorrow' was
their motto in times of unemployment and depression. One or
two music halls managed to survive, at LEEDS where Charlie

Chaplin once appeared in a turn called 'Lancashire Lass', and at NEWCASTLE which has enjoyed a revival of this type of entertainment back in the pubs where it began. No industrial area has a stronger tradition of local songs and ballads as pub entertainment than Tyneside—'The Colliers' Rant', 'Aw wish pay day Friday wad come', 'The Keel Row', 'Blaydon Races', 'Joe the Carrier's Lad', 'Keep your feet still, Geordie Hinny'—or a more esoteric routine of wisecracks and consciously Victorian atmosphere.

༄

There are no strippers to be seen at Balmbra's. This is pure self-conscious Victoriana with Tyneside accessories—a jockey's shirt which regularly appeared at Blaydon, a framed manuscript bearing a few bars of the song, portraits of local worthies. The entertainment is at its most daring when a bevy of girls do the can-can; otherwise the routine is a baritone singing 'Joe the Carrier's Lad', a soprano breaking off bits of 'Lilac Time' and a lightning artist with coloured chalks and sporadic patter. The thing that really holds the show up is the performance of the link-man . . . 'We have a smashing show for you tonight, lads and lasses. Our manager was out on his bicycle this morning scouring the four corners of the earth looking for talent. Yes, he went round the four corners of the earth. He went to Byker, West Heaton, Scotswood and Blaydon . . . And now we have Joe Bloggs, who's going to sing to you all. Joe's a canny lad with a tremendous reputation. He's sung before most of the Dukes of the realm. He's sung in front of the Duke of Norfolk, the Duke of Windsor, the Duke of Northumberland, and all the other pubs along the Scotswood Road.' The local jest that was devised by the first comic to tread the variety stage still brings the house down in Balmbra's.

Britain in the Sixties: The Other England, Geoffrey Moorhouse, 1964

༄

A clear sign of areas which have known bad times and conditions, when a decent meal or a job have been equally hard to come by, is the food fixation—leading to occasional orgies. One thinks of Lancashire fondness for the cheaper local specialities, tripe and trotters, black puddings of BURY, currant cakes of ECCLES, hot-pot suppers, the ubiquitous fish-and-chips or a 'dry fry' of potatoes, cockles and mussels, peas and pies, basins of carlings or grey peas and of 'burying them with ham'. Funeral teas are not all that different in enjoyment from wedding break-fasts once the ham stage has been succeeded by the trifle.

Holidays were rare occasions and slow to reach the northern factory worker : so pleasures had to be taken as they came. There was Whit Monday with its 'walks', when up to sixteen Friendly Societies marched in procession through BLACKBURN with a total following of four thousand people. These walks, chiefly of Sunday schools, Mothers' Unions, men's classes, ambulance brigades, and scouts are still a popular festival. Once the August Bank Holiday came on the statute book (1871) and special cheap excursions were run by the railways, a new reason arose for putting by the odd coppers throughout twelve months—a trip to the seaside. Rising at half-past four in the morning, spending six or seven hours in the shabbiest of trains, thirteen or fourteen to each carriage, standing, sitting on each other's knees or lying across rows of feet, the spinning operatives, tacklers and tenters, doffers, winders and side-piecers, the weavers, twisters, warp-dressers, mechanics, asbestos hands, stokers and clerks, all the grey and unnumbered multitude—made straight for air.

During the wakes season when whole towns, from Burslem and Macclesfield with its 'bumper Barnaby', to Huddersfield and Burnley, were depopulated for a week, everybody found his next door neighbour on the prom, the pier or the sand or in the pub at Blackpool, Scarborough, Bridlington, Skegness, South Shields or Whitley Bay unless they were at Llandudno, the snobs. When a northern town seemed asleep at seven or half past in a morning, mill gates stayed bolted and notices said 'No frying tonight', visitors knew that they had arrived on the annual holiday. 'Home from home' was usually a lodging-house where families 'found for themselves' and grumbled at the many rules.

Comic postcards flew back and forth. With their jokes about nagging mothers-in-law, mooning newly-weds, 'bird-fanciers', sharp landladies, red-nosed boozers and big bottoms in bathing costumes, they were, like the music-hall joke, a means of kicking over the traces for a brief interval, cocking-a-snook at prudery and sending a breezy message to those less fortunate stay-at-homes to show what the gay life does to you. Many of these comic cards are still produced in the same small West Riding town and in many a barber's or cobbler's or fish-and-chip shop a collection of them stuck on the wall enlivens bleaker days. Even the one-day 'chara' trips and works outings call for them, and the latest fads of female fashion are always burlesqued.

The contrast between leisure enjoyment for employees and their families and for families of the employers in the mid-century would have been ludicrous if it were not also pathetic. Daughters of the millowner, living at first in the spotlessly kept house within the mill precincts, later in the mansion or Gothic villa in a suburb beyond the worst smoke, were at a loss how to spend time. The tacit tribute to a man's effort and success was that his womenfolk should not engage in any materially useful occupation; they must acquire elegant accomplishments. So girls

> . . . drew costumes
> From French engravings . . . washed in
> Landscapes from nature (rather say, washed out),
> Danced the polka and Cellarius,
> Spun glass, stuffed birds, and modelled flowers in wax,
> Learnt cross-stitch . . .
> Producing what? A pair of slippers, sir,
> To put on when you're weary—or a stool
> To stumble over and vex you . . . 'curse that stool'.
> The poor club exercised her Christian gifts
> Of knitting stockings . . . the book club
> Preserved her intellectual. She lived
> A sort of cage-bird life, born in a cage.

That with reading aloud to the family, paying calls and a little lady-like gardening—following hints in the *Ladies' Companion to the Flower Garden*—made up her day. 'I may as well garden a bit. It will pass the time, and oh! how slow it is going.' So fetching her gloves and little mat Nell started to rake and weed among the crown imperials and sweet nancies, the nemophilas and sweet williams, fending off boredom.

'Play'—if he had cared to use such a term—for the manu-facturer, at his mill at six each morning and busy over his accounts until late evening, meant entertaining so that he could impress his guests with the lavishness of his table, the weight of his silver, the cost of his heavy gold-framed pictures. He had little time for the arts, although if he 'got on' he would endow a local library or an institute; he had little contact with intellectual affairs. *Laboro ergo sum* was his maxim. His like can still be met among provincial city aldermen, one of whom recently vetoed an Arts Council exhibition for a northern public gallery as 'indecent'—some Modigliani nudes were included in it. Assurance may, but culture does not, 'sit like a silk hat on a Bradford millionaire', when 'addling brass' is man's main justification to his Maker.

The term 'playing' used by a Northern workman often echoes a similar attitude. By 'playing' or 'laking' he means, 'not working', and not working in the past was too often a matter of compulsion, 'short time' or being 'laid off', rather than choice. 'Enforced leisure' in the 1920s and 30s was a traumatic experience for all who saw or endured it. Then, on a walking tour in the dales with knapsack and old clothes, the writer was asked 'Are you seeking work, lad?' sympathetically. Employment for the younger man meant five and a half days in spinning mill or weaving shed, a threepenny seat in a picture theatre twice a week, perhaps a ninepenny or shilling Saturday night dance, a Sunday afternoon parade on the road alongside the public park—then work again, and so on until he married. Unemployment—'playing'—meant 'Nothing to do with time: nothing to spend: nothing to do tomorrow or the day after: nothing to wear: can't get married'.

> Hands in pockets, shoulders hunched he would slink round the by-streets to the billiard hall, glad to be somewhere out of the way of the public gaze, any place where there were no girls to see him in his threadbare jacket and patched overalls. . . . 'I may as well be in blurry prison.' He suddenly wakened to the fact that he was a prisoner. The walls of the shops, houses and places of amusement were his prison walls. Walls and doors guarding him from the things he wanted. Where can a man go who hasn't any money? (Walter Greenwood).

To meet this situation of 'enforced leisure' a plan was thought up for establishing social centres for the working man. The Prince

of Wales touring TYNESIDE depressed areas where such leisure
often lasted five years, visited some of them : 'Dreary places, unused public halls, makeshift wooden structures often ill-lit and
shabbily furnished with hard benches and tables. The walls were
bare except for coloured lithographs of my parents and other
national figures'. A reproachful silence greeted his visits to these
rooms, the silence of men in despair.

Distraction for the working man may fulfil a double purpose.
As beer and cheap gin were the unspoken price with which the
busy Gradgrinds and Bounderby's reconciled the proletariat to
laissez faire conditions of employment and social misery, they were
also a means of dissipating his energy and bemusing his faculties
for organized protest and revolt. When gin went out sport came
in—the manipulated or commercialised sport of Cup Ties and
Cricket Championships, big 'fights', flat racing and dog tracks,
followed by hundreds of thousands in massed stadia with endless
Press or radio commentary. These fixtures differ, like 'tasty' cheese
from chalk, from the home-bred sport of the Lancashire cotton
belt, the cricket played from 1890 onwards by fourteen clubs
spread around Burnley—Nelson, Colne, Bacup, East Lancashire,
Church, Haslingden, Ramsbottom, Enfield, Lowerhouse, Accrington, Rawtenstall, Rishden, Burnley itself and, odd man out, Todmorden—where victory attacking batsmen on bowlers' wickets
make the genteel, style-before-everything, off-the-back-foot-defen-
sively-push-prod-poke stuff of the MCC type look to local devotees
too effete to live.

The league-table mania, the 'pools', the betting shops for those
who seldom or never set foot on a racecourse, the proliferation of
'Bingo' halls, the lavish TV coverage of national and international
sporting events—all boosted by massive advertising and publicity,
all appear to be officially condoned if not actively connived at or
encouraged. Football, no longer a seasonal game, is 'plugged' the
whole year through. All these offer an opiate, a vicarious chance
of action, excitement, 'winnings', to a working class that might
otherwise use its newfound leisure to explore the root causes and
cures of its underprivilege. That this state of affairs is not
accidental remains unprovable—the Roman state knew it as

'bread and circuses for the people'—but at all events, centralised, commercialised and passive 'sport' fits well into the pattern of the mass-production era and dense urban populations. For so many, today, instead of vigour and initiative in play or work, there can only be conditioned response—although sometimes, as in the ferocious 'effing and blinding' and bottle throwing at Everton, it exceeds calculations.

꧁꧂

Thirty-five thousand men and boys have just seen what most of them call 't'United' play Bolton Wanderers. . . . To say that these men paid their shillings to watch twenty-two hirelings kick a ball is merely to say that a violin is wood and catgut, that 'Hamlet' is so much paper and ink. For a shilling the Bruddersford United A.F.C. offered you Conflict and Art; it turned you into a critic, happy in your judgment of fine points, ready in a second to estimate the worth of a well-judged pass, a run down the touch-line, a lightning shot, a clearance kick by back or goal-keeper; it turned you into a partisan, holding your breath when the ball came sailing into your own goal-mouth, ecstatic when your forwards raced away towards the opposite goal, elated, downcast, bitter, triumphant by turns at the fortunes of your side. . . . It offered you more than a shilling's worth of material for talk during the rest of the week. A man who had missed the last home match of 't'United' had to enter social life on tiptoe in BRUDDERSFORD.

The Good Companions, J. B. Priestley, 1929

꧁꧂

This does not imply that the opportunities of a shorter working week and longer holidays, of better pay and education, of playing fields and recreation centres either municipal or management-provided, are not enjoyed and put to good use in the Northern industrial areas. Many get well away from Butlins and 'beat' and bingo to enjoy again fishing or fell-racing, whippet-training, 'rinkers' or local cricket and soccer. 'The English common people after hard work will go in the evening to football, stockball, cricket, prison-base, wrestling, cudgel playing or some such vehement exercise' is a statement only less generally true today than in 1660 when John Chamberlayne made it. Before the last war swarms of weekend cyclists started streaming out of the smoke-hung towns into open dales and moorland. The first major expansion of rock-climbing in Britain came during the 30s when young men from SHEFFIELD and MANCHESTER escaped from the emasculating experience of dole queues and short time working to the gritstone edges of Derbyshire. Now, from Derbyshire to Durham, there are cave and pothole, climbing and camping enthusiasts who seek to remake their leisure in adventurous terms, whether in clubs and groups or as 'lone tigers'.

༺ၹ຺

The illusion that life in northern cities and towns is necessarily dull dies hard.

But what is life in BRADFORD like? Outside one's job what are the rewards that Bradford can offer as a home town?

This is a long story, but first it is essential to dispel the cloth-cap image of a day that has long gone. How it has survived in an age of mass communication and mass merchandising is a miracle, but survive it does—an anachronism that does Bradford a disservice. Fashionwise—and fashion is perhaps the best comparative medium of all—Bradford is as smart as LONDON, and it isn't all on the back. Culturally, and in the world of music particularly, one has often felt that the north has sometimes had the edge on the south, with an appreciation of the real rather than the superficial things of life. This is borne out, surely, by the extraordinary variety of activity and interest revealed by the list of Bradford organisations. In Bradford, like interests quickly breed a strong community spirit, and it is this spirit of get-togetherness that makes Bradford so welcoming to the newcomer.

City of Bradford guide

The activities listed take up seven pages of the guide and include athletics, bee-keeping, canary clubs, drama groups, esperanto, gliding, judo, politics, rifle clubs, swimming, theosophy and vocal unions.   ༺ၹ຺

No one who knows LANCASHIRE and YORKSHIRE will doubt that finer faculties have their exercise also. Lancashire characters, hard workers all and not given any of them to wasting time, described the ways they used their leisure as 'recreations' or 'hobbies'. Music was the recreation of hundreds of Lancashire men from the school-master to the 'knocker-up'. These men did not make music from an aesthetic point of view much different from the aesthetic point of view passionately held by pigeon-fanciers. 'Listen to me, you bass-siz, get yo'r chest full for "And the Government" and follow mi beat' (Neville Cardus), the choirmaster would say. What they missed in appreciation of music's abstract form and pattern, they made up in drawing out tone and expression.

The Messiah and Cresswell colliery band, the Mikado, the 'little theatre', pigeon-racing and Pudsey & District Chrysan-themum Society—all form part of play here : an old wool ware-house in Bradford still bears on its peeling signboard the name Delius.

TRADE

'*If everybody minded their own business,*' the Duchess said in a hoarse growl, '*the world would go round a deal faster than it does.*'

Alice's Adventures in Wonderland, Lewis Carroll, 1865

Geordie, if anybody tells thou he's a millionaire, then tell him he's robbed some poor bugger.

Pit-Yacker, George Hitchin, 1962

Up to the beginning of the Second World War it was said of business circles on Merseyside that 'decent chaps owned ships, fairly decent chaps broked cotton, almost decent chaps broked corn—the rest just did not exist'. In a simplified form there lies the reason for Britain's old supremacy in world trade and her later accelerating decline.

Concentration on staple trades—of which cotton was long the major one—ability to convey exports to all continents in merchant ships—of which Britain was the world's chief builder—opportunity to bring raw materials and foodstuffs, via ports such as Liverpool, from her colonies not only to her own but to European markets (with the additional gain of shipping dues), all these added up to an apparently invincible economic position. A century ago it was no idle boast that Britain was chief exporter, chief consumer and chief organiser in world trade.

What happened to change this fortunate situation, with its specially unfortunate effect on the industrial North of England? To see clearly the main causes and consequences of trade decline depends upon reviewing first the course of Britain's remarkable trade ascendancy: and against this background can be judged the subsequent story of strikes.

111

Foremost in time and in long-term value was the acquisition of overseas territories: Jamaica, captured by Cromwell in 1655 with other West Indian islands to follow; Gibraltar, a trade route bastion, taken in 1704; Canada, won from the French in 1763; large tracts of India, occupied by the East India Company (founded 1600) in the course of the war with the French; thirteen colonies along the coast of North America, British until 1776; a number of settlements along the coast of West Africa; a claim on the continent of Australia made possible by Cook's voyage in 1769-71. The importance of these acquisitions as sources of foodstuffs, raw materials and markets for manufactured goods, was equalled only by their value to British merchants with capital to invest, to the shipowners and, later, the railway development companies. Timber, tobacco, sugar, corn, jute, wool were some of the raw materials at British disposal. Under the laws of the old colonial system many of the most prized materials could only pass into Europe via British ports, whilst trade between Britain and her colonies was only carried on in British or colonial ships. The manufacture of certain goods, woollens in particular, came at first under restriction in the colonies for the greater benefit of British home interests.

The Empire continued to grow. Against commercial losses incurred both in India and the West Indies, as a result of conflict with the French, and the upset to economy following the abolition of the slave trade, could be set new sources of gain—Ceylon, Trinidad, Tobago, Malta, the Cape of Good Hope—acquired in the Peace Treaty of 1815. These were but the beginnings of a growth which before the century was half over embraced South Africa, New Zealand and two-thirds of the continent of India.

Britain also added a head-start in the techniques of industry to the advantage of her territories abroad, her shipping and shipping routes protected by a powerful navy, her rich sources of raw materials. The long war with France, with its demands for munitions and for uniforms, had led to rapid expansion of the iron industry and stimulated invention of labour-saving equipment in textiles. Its aftermath may have brought temporary depression, less demand at home for those products and less

Work: Forge: engraving by T. Sharples, enginesmith 1829-93

Work: English steel

Work: (above) Old style trimmers; (below) Modern steelworkers

Work: Britain's first automated colliery

Play: (above) Fairground, South Shields. . . ; (below) and beach party

Play: (left) Young vigour and (below) Older skill

Play: (left) With the crowd

(below) And away from it

Play: Fanciers

Trade: (above) Cloth Hall, Leeds; (below) Clothing factory, Wigan

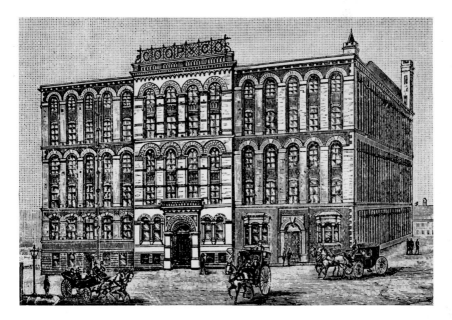

Trade: Cotton magnate's gift hall, Todmorden

Trade: Shipyard, Sunderland

Trade: (left) Yard closed, Jarrow

(below) End of a pottery

Trade: Production

demand still from customers abroad exhausted by the struggle, but in industrialisation Britain stood well in advance of her rivals. Trade lost in Europe could be gained in the New World and in the South American colonies, taken from Spain and Portugal after the war. So, with her natural resources of coal and iron, her adaptable manpower and *laissez-faire* system, Britain moved into a period of unchallenged trade supremacy.

In the course of two mid-century decades, coal output doubled, from 45,000,000 to over 100,000,000 tons annually; iron output was trebled in twenty years, then doubled again, rising from 1,000,000 to 6,000,000 tons; shipping tonnage leapt up from 3,000,000 to 5,000,000, with two of those five million in steam, as well as the famous clippers and iron ships coming off the stocks to fight off the American merchantmen's challenge. Thanks to Bessemer's process, cheap steel brought that industry's output from 40,000 tons a year to 1,250,000 in less than a generation, and for the proliferating railways proved invaluable.

The greatest trading commodities were few and in their production the North of England was paramount. Cotton came easily first. Imported as raw material from America in a tonnage rising from a modest 25,000 to almost 350,000 from the beginning to the mid-century, it topped the list of exports and was shipped, in finished goods, to America, India and Africa. In less than thirty years the number of Manchester's spinning mills rose from fifty-two to ninety-nine : in the five years 1835-40 out of a total official export of about £50,000,000 value annually, almost £24,000,000 was in cotton goods. Woollens and worsteds came second—with an annual total of £6,000,000. Australia became the greatest source of raw wool and the mills of the West Riding were voracious in their demand; exports of mixed wool and cotton fabrics from the Riding expanded from 2,400,000 to 42,115,000 yards between 1839 and 1849. Together, textiles made up sixty per cent of the export total : right up to 1913 one-third of all British exports were textiles, with Lancashire supplying two-thirds of the world's cotton exports. The superiority of British machinery and organisation enabled this country to maintain her export lead in spite of wage increases and reduction in hours of labour.

G

The see-saw effect of almost total dependence on a single source of raw material hit home, however, during the American Civil War, when blockade of the cotton ports of the Southern states led to idling in most Lancashire mills, large-scale unemployment and near starvation. (Even so, principle came before interest and the 'silent example' of Lancashire workers deterred the Government of the day from supporting the South and slavery against Lincoln and the North.)

After textiles in volume came the trade in coal, iron and steel, and machinery. Coal, exported mainly to Europe, and iron formed the staple industries of Durham and Northumberland, with important non-phosphoric iron also from west Cumberland: steel and machinery had their prominent centres in Sheffield and Manchester. The speed of Sheffield's jump into heavy industry in the first half of the nineteenth century can be gathered from the town's growth from a comparatively small settlement to a population of 135,000 by 1851. Much of the rapid advance in the export of machinery depended on the machine tool makers Joseph Bramah, of Barnsley, Henry Maudslay, son of a Yorkshire migrant to Woolwich Arsenal, and his pupils James Nasmyth and Joseph Whitworth, who began in Manchester in the 30s the manufacture of such things as standardised gauges, measuring machines, classified screws and screw threads, all of vital importance in the saving of time, labour and exporters' reputation.

୧ଦ୪ବ

That 'ferruginous person' the 'iron gentleman', Mr Rounce-well, remarks, in apology for a hasty visit to Chesney Wold: 'In these busy times, when so many great undertakings are in progress, people like myself have so many workmen in so many places, that we are always on the flight. . . .'

'And it is a remarkable example of the confusion into which the present age has fallen, of the obliteration of landmarks, the opening of floodgates, and the uprooting of distinctions', says Sir Leicester Dedlock with stately gloom, 'that I have been informed that he (the ironmaster) has been invited to go into Parliament . . . which is fraught with strange considerations, —startling considerations as it appears to me'.

Bleak House, Charles Dickens, 1853

Less than a century later the ironmaster Baldwin was to be three times Prime Minister.

❧

By 1860 there was no question about Great Britain's position as 'workshop of the world' as well as the world's chief trader, nor about the industries which reinforced her position. The development of her economy was not only via the shipping routes and markets overseas, but in home fields also.

❧

Viewed in the light of the town's subsequent growth the most important events to occur in BRADFORD during the eighteenth century were those of the 1770's . . . the first of these events was the passing of an Act authorising the construction of a canal between LEEDS and LIVERPOOL to pass along the Aire valley within three miles of BRADFORD. This canal was essentially a BRADFORD project . . . the original idea probably stemmed from Longbottom, a pupil of Smeaton and Brindley, but it was promptly taken up by John Hustler, a Quaker woolstapler and one of BRADFORD's leading citizens. The first general meeting of those interested in the scheme was held neither at LEEDS nor LIVERPOOL, but at the Sun Inn, BRADFORD and henceforward BRADFORD was at the centre of the affairs of the Company. The head office remained in BRADFORD until 1850 : of the capital subscribed BRADFORD was, after LONDON, the greatest single source.

By 1777 the canal was open for traffic. Not only the town's main industry, but other enterprises were stimulated. Coal mined around BRADFORD was exported to SKIPTON, KEIGHLEY and the CRAVEN district. In return the barges brought limestone to be smelted in BRADFORD : some went later to the Low Moor and Bowling iron works for use as a flux.

Bradford Textile Society Journal, 1953-4

❧

Just as the building of canals as a method of industrial transport in the late eighteenth century had contributed much to the expansion of the coal, iron, textile and pottery trade in Lancashire and the West Riding and in north Staffordshire, so in the middle years of the nineteenth century the great increase of railway mileage, from about 2,000 to 14,000, besides making vast demands on the coal and iron industries, speeded up trade and business. It also furthered the building of new towns and therefore new markets in an era when Britain's population showed a twenty-five per cent increase (census 1851 and 1871). Many of the canals were then bought out by railway companies, to fall into subsequent disuse : those towns, like Stoke-on-Trent, which had preferred to rely on canal transport and kept away the main line railways, soon exchanged complacency for regret. The export trade, of course, also profited hugely when raw cotton and wool could be carried from port to mill, textile goods from mill to port, coal from pit to factory and business men from city to city at speeds advancing from the statutory minimum of twelve mph (Railways Act, 1844) to averages of nearly seventy mph by the end of the century. And, by inevitable logic, as the needs of foreign trade mounted so ship-building increased until Great Britain's output of ships was greater than that of all other nations together.

ᗡᗡᗡ

The real start of large-scale public railways was the LIVERPOOL to MANCHESTER line to which Stephenson was appointed engineer in 1826. . . . In the Rainhill Trial of 1829 Stephenson's 'Rocket' which reached a speed of 30 mph won the prize for locomotives. . . . In 1830 the line was opened. It was immediately successful and its success settled all doubts about the use of steam locomotives. It carried a great passenger traffic during the first few years, far more than had been anticipated : and it stimulated a rush to promote railway companies, get private Acts of Parliament passed and start building the lines. By 1843 there were also lines from NEWCASTLE to CARLISLE, DARLINGTON to RUGBY, LIVERPOOL to HULL, and DERBY to GLOUCESTER, besides other smaller ones. The era of railway building had been fairly launched.

British Economic and Social History, 1700-1939, C. P. Hill, 1961

It remains axiomatic that to reach or view the industrial heart of a northern town one travels by rail : look, for instance at the vistas of works and their intimate structures beside the track at Warrington or Leeds, or Thornaby-on-Tees.

ᗡᗡᗡ

The benefits of expanding trade almost everywhere in this high noon of Victorian enterprise were felt first by the middle-class manufacturers, the mill-masters whose works were deemed large if they employed 250 hands. Except in banking, shipping, some iron and steel concerns and the railways, family partnership was the general rule. The partners took a direct interest in the works and the efficient workman had a reasonable chance of notice and promotion. (As early as 1800 Robert Owen had risen from haberdasher's shop assistant at £25 per year via Manchester cotton-machinery making and spinning to manager of a mill with a salary of £1,000—enormous for those days.) In the third quarter of the century 'real wages' were to rise by about one-third, unless the workman happened to be a general labourer or docker : the wages of skilled men such as engineers more than kept pace with rising prices. Consumption of tea, sugar, meat and tobacco rose in working-class families, a sure index. Cotton manufacturers,[1] needless to say, made fortunes without quenching their desire to make even bigger ones—as other captains of the textile industry were to do later. In the dormitory suburbs of some northern textile towns one may still see the late nineteenth-century mansions of what is jocularly called 'millionaires' row'.

One section of society, however, benefited out of all proportion—as a result of a new Act, passed in 1862—and at the same time began to divorce business success from responsibility for business practices. The Companies Act, conferring on joint-stock companies the privilege of limited liability, gave the chance to financiers of transferring their credit and freedom of commercial action to others, while amassing a personal fortune in shares, or of promoting new enterprises not for long-term production but for quick capital appreciation. With the extension of machinery and transport, industry was constantly increasing the scale of its operations and so needed more and more capital; organised capital made nonsense of individual concern and personal responsibility. The company promoter, raising money on loan to float or purchase commercial concerns, could escape if they collapsed before

---

[1] A Cheshire muslin manufacturer, Samuel Oldknow, was reputed to be earning £17,444 a year before 1800.

a profitable selling time was reached, under cover of limited liability—leaving credulous shareholders to bear the burden. Thus a man without conscience could grow immensely rich and, at a time when the landed gentleman was being replaced in Parliament by the successful financier, immensely powerful in addition.

Mr Merdle, a man of prodigious enterprise 'was in everything good, from banking to building. He was in Parliament, of course. He was in the City necessarily. The weightiest of men had said to projectors, "Now, what name have you got? Have you got Merdle?" And the reply being in the negative, had said, "Then I won't look at you." ' His death in a warm bath, with an empty laudanum bottle and a tortoise-shell handled penknife, is put about at first as being due to 'pressure'—not to the real complaint, according to Dickens, 'forgery and robbery'. 'Numbers of men in every profession and trade would be blighted by his insolvency; old people who had been in easy circumstances all their lives would have no place of repentance for their trust in him but the workhouse; legions of women and children would have their whole future desolated by the hand of this mighty scoundrel. Every partaker of his magnificent feasts would be seen to have been a sharer in the plunder of innumerable homes.' In fact this bargain-driver with a Minister for Lordships of the Circumlocution Office had sprung from nothing, had never had any money of his own, his ventures had been utterly reckless and his expenditure most enormous.

Mr Merdle's successor is Sir Georgias Midas, the company promoter in Du Maurier's drawings of later Victorian society. The title 'millionaire'—which Richard Arkwright, the first great factory owner had almost claimed—began to smell. Profitability, as sole criterion in business, whether it was Merdle-projected or not, was a bad substitute for conscience. It left the workman's job and security to depend on circumstances completely outside his control, among great combines and corporations remote from the ethos of 'paternal management'.

But even in the high noon of prosperity there were signs of change on the horizon. Already, in the 1840s, when Canada became a self-governing dominion, one of her first independent acts had been to pass a tariff of duties against British goods. The growth of Free Trade policies, demanded by most merchants and manufacturers at home, had caused the cessation of Colonial Preference towards her timber and wheat, and so Canada entered also into a Reciprocity Treaty with the USA to open that market for her commodities. A move of a different kind in the Free Trade campaign—the French treaty of 1860 (signed by Cobden, cotton spinner) by which all import duties on silk goods were abolished —caused wide distress in the home silk industry. Handloom capacity in Macclesfield fell from 6,000 to 2,000; only silk throwing maintained the industry under threat from foreign competition in silk weaving.

A different tempo in the flow of trade was already becoming plain—to compare with the time when the pushing merchants of Liverpool had hauled so fast ahead of the genteel merchants of older centres such as Bristol :

> We came back to LIVERPOOL, got luncheon and went to see the docks. Nothing gives one so vivid an idea of the vast commerce of the country as these docks, quays and immense warehouses, piled and cumbered with hides, cotton, tallow, corn, oil-cake, wood and wine, oranges and other fruit and merchandise of all kinds from all corners of the world. I admired the dray horses very much, huge creatures seventeen or eighteen hands high, more like elephants than horses.
> Fifteen, ten and even five years ago there was much more trade and wealth in Liverpool and much larger fortunes more rapidly made than now. There has been of late and there still is a stagnation of trade, a depression and deterioration of credit. Formerly the streets were blocked by the enormous business and the mountains of merchandise passing about, but there is plenty of room now.
>   Diary, Rev Francis Kilvert, 20 June 1872

The real challenge to Britain—always with her historic rivals France, Holland, Spain—came from new competitors, Germany and America. British engineers and constructing companies had built railways in nearly every developing country in the world, but America was to build her own, taking only rails and some equipment from Britain. Then the opening up of the prairies for wheat, of the western grazing lands for beef cattle, coupled with the discovery of vast iron and coal resources, gave America a huge trade in foodstuffs abroad and at the same time upset Britain's semi-monopolist position in steel. Germany also, having acquired rich ironfields in Lorraine as a result of the Franco-Prussian war (1870-71), rapidly built up her steel industry. Within twenty-five years of that war's end not only had America overtaken British production of steel, but so had Germany—ironically by using the British Gilchrist-Thomas process which complemented Bessemer's in converting phosphoric iron ores. By the end of the century these two countries together were producing three times the amount of Britain's output, although her exports of steel still exceeded theirs. Again both countries erected tariff barriers to protect their own manufactures, whilst Britain maintained free trade.

Yet the most serious threat to Britain's supremacy arose from the fact that new inventions were rendering much of the older plant out of date and there had to be heavy writing-off in equipment. As in certain other of her basic industries later, Britain suffered from having been first in the field, whilst her challengers could start with up-to-date plant and machinery without having capital tied-up in the obsolescent.

'Trade follows the flag' is a catch-phrase of which at first the reverse was more true. International competition for foreign markets, 'concessions' and spheres of interest, with Germany, France, Belgium, Italy and Portugal all taking part, created a situation in which Britain, so largely dependent on world-wide export trade, found herself almost bound to play a leading role. From individual trading enterprises, exploration and the activities of chartered companies formed by British shareholders, colonies were established under Crown control. Africa offered the greatest of these opportunities: in addition to the acquisitions there of her rivals, Britain added some 5,000,000 square miles of African territory to her Empire within a single generation, including Nigeria, Kenya and Rhodesia. Other spheres of interest were Egypt, Fiji, Malaya and the Chinese ports: soon after the turn of the century Britain also laid hands on the gold of the Transvaal. British trade thus enjoyed a double stimulus: more new markets for manufactured goods and heavy equipment, like rails, engines, mining machinery, steamships; more and new raw materials, such as rubber, tin, vegetable oils, aluminium.

Although the new raw materials were grist to her rivals' mills also, there was obviously ample area for growth and enterprise in British trade. Until the last decade of the nineteenth century, in fact, Britain's foreign trade remained greater in total than that of her two major rivals combined, even if her rate of expansion did not come up to theirs. Britain's markets were still in America, Germany and Europe generally, but India, New Zealand, Australia, Canada were her best markets. The total tonnage of British steamships mounted steadily from just under the 2,000,000 already noted to over 11,000,000 in the course of forty years; from 1912 onwards, conversion to oil-burning was not to be a factor in Britain's favour in competition with America. The opening of the Manchester Ship Canal in 1893 allowed ocean-going steamers to dock in the commercial capital of the north : in less than twenty years the city became fourth port in the kingdom in terms of the value of traffic handled.

In all this there was one disquieting change of direction. It was becoming more difficult for Britain to sell manufactured goods. Instead of Lancashire cottons and Yorkshire woollens, the old foundations of export success, the proportionate place of these goods was being taken over by ships, coal and machinery. With these plus their own raw materials many of Britain's customers were enabled to turn themselves into her competitors. Such exceptions as the export of 'wool tops', semi-finished goods to countries that regarded these semi-manufactures as raw materials for their own industries, only proved the rule.

❧

Exports 1880-84	Value in millions
Textiles	£108
	(Cotton £76)
Iron, steel, coal	£38
Machinery	£15
Clothing	£10

(In 1881 Britain could have bought £50,000,000 more of imports than the value of the goods exported, partly through her invisible exports.)

Exports 1913	*Value in* *millions*
Cotton goods	£127
Woollen goods	£38
Coal and coke	£54
Iron and steel	£54
Machinery	£37

(Exports of coal, iron and steel had climbed steeply, but cotton still remained one-third of the export value total.)

The Evolution of Modern Industry, F. R. Jervis, 1960

In 1900 Britain's share of world trade amounted to	33%
1939	22%
1963	15%

ᥫᩣ

The crippling blow of war fell—but its full crippling action was delayed until the war itself was over. Britain became cut off from many of her sources of supply and overseas markets: countries to whom she exported certain goods either turned elsewhere for them or began to develop their manufacture at home. Coal, iron, steel, shipbuilding and engineering, of course, had a boom period; cotton, wholly dependent on imported material and not in such wartime demand as woollen goods, suffered badly. While steel production was rising by fifty per cent, one function of the Cotton Control Board, set up under wartime emergency, was to fix the maximum percentage of machinery that each mill might work so as to ration the cotton available. All in all, apart from immense disruption of labour, depreciation of plant—especially in coal mining—and interruption of raw material supply, the effect of war upon Britain was a drop of forty-five per cent in the volume of her export trade compared with 1913. The burden of having to pay a huge war debt to America and the risk of being paid reparations by Germany in goods did nothing to facilitate recovery.

Post-war trade could not return to normalcy because conditions had changed. Contraction of the coal, iron and steel, shipbuilding and engineering markets to peacetime needs, could not be matched by expansion in other traditional Northern industries, when India and Japan were building their own mills and selling their own cheap cotton products throughout the Far East. Coal exporters also had to face the rise of mining industries in other countries, the use of hydro-electric power by former customers and the change-over to oil-burning at sea. 'Here's a piece of coal as black as muck, I hope it brings the best o' luck'—Durham miners' traditional New Year greeting brought luck at this time limited to the strikes and difficulties experienced in America and Germany, which only allowed a temporary recovery of British trade. Steel and iron were in for a black decade, with much unwanted plant that had been extended during the war at high cost, naval construction severely reduced and the British carrying trade affected by merchant marine services built up by rivals. Even so cotton was worst hit. Many cotton mills had been the victims of the company promoter and recapitalised at high value in a brief 1920 boom, caused by the demand for goods immediately after the war. When Lancashire found that she had lost to Japan the export market in India, the trade she retained in quality goods was only a small proportion of her expected heritage. By 1930 exports to India had fallen to the extent of 1,000,000,000 yards. The overseas markets for woollen goods were also shrinking, but that industry suffered less from the fact of its greater reliance on home sales.

These peacetime blows fell particularly heavily on the North. For almost ten years the volume of Britain's exports was to remain below the 1913 level and in south Lancashire, on the north-east coast and Clydeside, unemployment became a permanent fact of life. In itself unemployment is a wasting disease. Although no economist can suppose that when the loss of foreign markets set 2,000,000 men out of work 'those two million are any more to blame than the people who draw blanks in the Calcutta Sweep', many of the miners and weavers who had been brought up to work were ashamed of being unemployed.

So long as Bert Jones across the street is still at work, Alf Smith, unemployed, is bound to feel himself dishonoured and a failure.

Hence that frightful feeling of impotence and despair which is almost the worst evil of unemployment—far worse than any hardship, worse than the demoralisation of enforced idleness, and only less bad than the physical degeneracy of Alf Smith's children born on the P.A.C. (George Orwell).

Chronic depression was a state of mind as well as a state of trade in Britain's older staple industries, on which her economic supremacy had been built.

After the stock exchange crash of October 1929 hit America, the Great Depression of the early 30s in Britain led to a fall in industrial production of some sixteen per cent in two years and a critical stage in chronic unemployment of over three million out of work. At the worst point the shipbuilding industry, for example, had only thirty-seven per cent of its workers in employment; in Jarrow, after the closure of Palmer's shipyard, unemployment was the fate of seventy-two per cent. The Jarrow Crusade which so excited public sympathy saw a march by 200 unemployed men to London with a petition from Jarrow 'anxiously praying that HM Government realise the urgent need that work be provided for the town . . . . that they may be relieved of their present distress and misery and may look forward to the future with trust and dignity.'

The way of recovery for Britain was inevitably slow. It lay in the use of new materials and the development of new industries in which other countries had often made a head start, and this in a European situation when nations were either seeking their own economic self-sufficiency, imposing quotas to limit their imports of certain goods or else suffering from inflation. The newer industries such as artificial silk, plastics, motor-car manufacture, electric and wireless equipment did not require coalfields, but used electricity as source of power. They tended to concentrate in the south Midlands or in the towns of the Thames valley closer to the great consumer area of London. Much of their production was for the home market. They did not need men who had grown to the habit of the skills required for heavy industry. British tariffs, which were now imposed on imported iron and steel goods (Import Duties Act 1932), and quota agreements helped recovery, as also did the Ottawa preferential agreements with the dominions for manufactured goods, but it was from the newer iron centre of the Midlands that three-fifths of home production came. While the rest of the country could at any rate look forward to a more prosperous and comfortable future, the older industrial areas still had to fight off decline. The north-east coast and west Cumberland were officially designated 'depressed areas' (later graduating to 'distressed', then to 'special' areas).

⟨∞⟩

In the year to March, 1967, the Cumberland area produced 662,000 tons of coal. This coal was sold at an average price of 123s 6d a ton and the area made a loss of 40s 1d for every ton produced. Combining these two figures gives 163s 3d as the average cost per ton.

Now it is known that the British coal industry has ample reserves that could be extracted, if required, at very low marginal cost.

If the NCB can produce extra or marginal tonnage at only 50s a ton then a loss of 113s 3d a ton is being made in this area. This average loss per ton on production of 662,000 tons gives a total loss of just less than £3.75 million.

The cost of Cumberland

In the Cumberland area the average number of workers employed by the NCB in the year in question was 3,300. If the Board is continuing mining operations purely because it does not wish to aggravate the rather serious unemployment problem in Cumberland then it is costing just under £1,150 a year for each man employed. This is the average subsidy per man which the NCB is effectively paying because it does not completely abandon coal production in Cumberland.

Sunday Times, 24 September 1967

⟨∞⟩

By 1937 national unemployment at last dropped below 1,500,000, industrial output had climbed twenty-five per cent from that of 1929, yet apart from iron and steel the older industries remained sick and the total of exports fell seventeen per cent short of its volume before the depression. Losses in old industries were not being offset by gains in new, where other countries had still an international lead. Only the Second World War it seemed could supply stimulus strong enough to fend off the likelihood of another big depression, despite the significant, but slow shift from *laissez-faire* to State-managed economy.

'Silk has set Macclesfield at the top of the industrial ladder. Helping to keep it there are those industries which have little or nothing in common with the silk trade, but which are important both to the town's prosperity and as a defence against possible depression' *(Official Guide)*. Macclesfield, in fact, apart from producing specialist machinery, like other textile towns, soon adapted it to rayon (the manufacture of which expanded from £53,000,000 value to £120,000,000 between 1929 and 1939), then to the more sophisticated man-made fibres such as nylon and terylene. Through these products of the chemical industry its trade has become linked ever more closely with ICI. Even so the town has seen fit to diversify with cork and paper manufacture and recently with pharmaceutical chemicals. The key word, for trade, is diversification.

✿

Whitworth's armament and precision instrument works, MANCHESTER, originally established in 1833, moved to OPEN-SHAW in 1880, amalgamated with Armstrongs of NEWCASTLE-ON-TYNE in 1897, then merged with Vickers of BARROW and Cammell Laird of BIRKENHEAD in the 1920's to form the English Steel Corporation, the whole of the small tools and tool steel business being concentrated at OPENSHAW. After diversification moves into motor cars, tractors, hovercraft, and diesel engines Vickers are currently shedding their dependence on armaments and expensive plant in favour of medical equipment, printing machinery, synthetic fibre plant, malting and bottling equipment, and marzipan mixing plant in their attempts to climb out of a descending profit spiral.

Sunday Times Business News, July 1967

✿

In some older industries, such as Nottingham's lace-making, new machinery made it fairly easy to adapt from a declining fashion market to a soaring one such as artificial silk stockings, but the Batleys, the Jarrows and the Blackburns have seen that their trade salvation lay in finding as many baskets as possible for their industrial eggs. Batley and shoddy, Jarrow and ships, Blackburn and cotton have ceased to be synonymous. Blackburn has more workers now in light engineering and electronics than in cotton; Jarrovians produce chemicals, cigarette filters, acrylic knitting yarns and steel scaffolding as well as the great steel castings of old. The Team Valley industrial estate has produced 70,000 new jobs in two decades. The Tyne shipyards themselves are to be concentrated—'cutting down fat' they call it—in an attempt to save overheads, phase process work, speed construction and win orders. Batley has a finger in a dozen pies. . . . None of these places, however, can rival Bristol in diversification. No manufacturing concern there, except the aircraft company, employs anything like ten per cent of the working population. Its economy is more evenly spread than that of any other similar city in the country, its unemployment figures are consistently below the national average and its prosperity unquestioned.

The pattern of Northern trade has begun to change. To regain a prosperity on Merseyside, for instance, matching that of the modern Severnside, has meant revising the whole industrial structure. Ships, cotton, corn were clearly not enough (with the majority of workers employed in handling rather than producing) when for most of the last two decades unemployment stood at well over twice the national average. Liverpool, like Jarrow, sought powers by Act of Parliament to build new factories, establish industrial estates and make loans to industry when the supporting tripod of its commerce, transport and distribution began to 'give'. Nowadays car plants, electrical-appliance firms and various other skilled trades are offering work to families whose livelihood used to depend on one or two daughters sorting coupons for the pools. 'Decasualisation' of labour is an attempt, however unwelcome among the go-getters, to steady dockers' conditions and prospects.

❦

The industrial structure of Lancashire is now fairly healthy, if it is judged by its proportion of employment in the most rapidly growing industry groups. Between 1954 and 1959 the manufacturing groups with the greatest increase in production in Britain, in order of the size of the increase, were Vehicles, Chemicals, Other Manufacturing Industry, Engineering, Paper and Printing, Food, Drink and Tobacco, and 'Metal Goods Not Elsewhere Specified'. Only in the Vehicles and Metal Goods N.E.S. groups is the Lancashire proportion of total employment smaller than the proportion for Great Britain, and even this will change, for there are plans for a substantial growth in the assembly of motor cars in the Merseyside area.

So far as low-growth industries are concerned, Lancashire's main problem is textiles. In Lancashire's traditional industries, cotton and clothing, the small plant has been the rule. The change in the industrial structure has been eased by the successful location in Lancashire since the War—often in disused cotton mills—of new small plant trades, such as carton manufacture, electronic component manufacture, and food preparation industries. The new firms have suited the Textile areas in that they continue in the tradition of the small establishment and small firm that has so long been a feature of the cotton textile industry, especially in the weaving section.

(But) Lancashire is not what it was. In its population and industry it is now a less significant part of Britain.

Manchester and its Region, British Association Survey, 1962

∾

Trade in the North has come to depend less and less on fighting against losses in the old staple industries, for which former customers have developed their own natural resources or technical skill. Nor can it be the North's task, as in the past, to put Britain on top of the world market again—in a world changed by the independence of India and Africa, the take-over bids of America and progressive nationalisation of home industries, including steel: a world, moreover, where integration, not competition with Europe, seems the only way to ensure a scale of technological advance capable of holding off the USA at all. That the invention of the lady's bicycle reduced the demand for pianos is a truism of economics: the demand for a whole range of different products and the expansion of competing industries has changed if not reduced, the North's position, perhaps for good.

Along with the North's productive pre-eminence the new situation has put paid also to the 'lump o' labour' theory—the idea, often blamed upon trades unions, that there is only a fixed amount of employment to be had and that, therefore, the less any worker does, the more there will be for others to do. The less he does the less employment from export trade for all alike—so long as the figures produced in 1966 for six major industries (steel, chemicals, metal products, transport equipment, electrical and non-electrical machinery) continue to show that it takes from two to four Britons to produce what one man in certain overseas competing nations produces.

STRIKE

*Combination is an awful power. It is like the equally mighty
agency of steam: capable of almost unlimited good or evil.*

Mary Barton, a Tale of Manchester Life, Mrs Gaskell

*We've done with strike and lock-out—
They cause too many a knock-out;
We'll take to making laws O!
We'll take to making the laws!*

From Songs for Socialists, R. C. K. Ensor, 1912

*I would rather live under a Dey of Algiers than a trades com-
mittee.*

Richard Cobden

Workers' unions—or combinations—in the modern sense grew
up when craftsmen ceased to be the owners of the major tools of
their trade and under the industrial system there began a permanent dissociation between master and man. Parliament no
longer cared to or could apply the old statutes for ensur-
ing reasonable wages and conditions of employment—such as the
Elizabethan Statute of Apprentices—and the doctrine of *laissez
faire* left the employer free to do what he liked with his own. So
workers in the late eighteenth century found that their only course
was to fight for the right of collective bargaining. At first they
tried petition and appeal to the old statutes; later, when some
forty acts had been passed to outlaw trade combinations—
nominally because they infringed the power of the State—they
formed secret unions, convened under oath. With the safety valve
of union bargaining closed, outbreaks of violence—such as the
machine smashing of the Luddites—followed. When in 1824 the
Combination Acts were repealed the way was left clear again

for workers to choose their course of action and show the reasons for it publicly.

June 1825 saw in Bradford the beginning of a strike which might be called classic for its circumstances and pattern. In the worsted industry the prime motive for combination was workmen's opposition to new machinery. A combing machine had been tried in BRADFORD in 1794, unsuccessfully : power looms intended for use there had been removed under weavers' threats much more recently. Woolcombers, aware that their safety of employment depended only on the technical difficulties of developing suitable machines, and already well organised, now sought to form a joint union with the weavers. At that point an energetic Bradford mill master began to experiment with power looms : others, anxious not to be left behind in production and trade opportunities, followed his lead. The Woolcombers' & Stuffweavers' Union after taking prominent part in a public procession then asked for increases in wage rates, claiming that the wool being used was of higher quality and more difficult to comb. They also opposed the introduction of machinery to 'supercede their ancient art'.

The employers met to consider these claims—from $\frac{1}{4}$d in low quality to $\frac{1}{2}$d a pound more in the finer wools for combers, who as labour aristocrats earned 20s to 25s weekly, and rises ranging from 9d to 2s in their weekly earnings of 10s to 12s for weavers. To back their demand the Woolcombers' & Stuffweavers' Union threatened strikes. As soon as the masters rejected these demands the strike began, with talk of it lasting for six or seven years.

Strike action affected three firms only at first—those reputed to be the lowest wage payers. About fifty employers, pledging themselves not to employ any comber who continued to be a member of the union, came to their defence. When men brought work in they were offered the choice of dismissal or rejecting combination. Although consideration might be given to increasing weavers' wages the employers were out to crush the union. Both sides refused an offer of arbitration and within the month about 3,000 workers were unemployed, whilst 400 had left Brad-

ford for work elsewhere. The 'Great Strike' was causing much
hardship to workmen and their dependents, but men refused to
desert their union.

In the face of a threat of selective strikes by the workers the
employers next set about 'black-listing' union leaders and decided
to dismiss all children of union members. By the end of the second
month they had further resolved to stop all the mills—a general
'lock-out'. Half a dozen masters opted out of this (one firm even
granted the increases), but in August the rest were still insisting
that their combers and weavers and also the parents of child
workers must renounce the union. Various newspapers advised
conciliation, as the Tory county MP had done already, but on
6 August over thirty mills put the 'lock-out' into force and 43,000
spindles fell idle. Employers in other towns, from Leeds and
Halifax to Lancaster and Darlington, now gave their support in
the hope of starving union members into submission.

Arbitration was again offered and refused. The conflict
appeared as one between hand and power weaving, deemed
superior in its product by the masters. The union held rallies and
appealed for funds—it was having to spend over £100 daily on
benefits. From Hull, Huddersfield, Loughborough and London
donations poured in and the unionists remained confident. Because of the dispute other workers had now become unemployed,
to a total between 20,000 and 30,000; employers also in other
areas were dismissing union members as a token of common
action. When union collectors in several towns received their dismissal funds diminished and the WSWU's appeals for support
became worried and urgent.

By autumn the position of the unemployed had grown serious
and there were rumours of union secretaries pocketing funds.
Further support came from Sheffield and Manchester, but the
hold of the union leaders on Bradford's workers began to weaken.
The Times commented, tendentiously, that they had become great
public functionaries, lifted into high authority by the combination, to whom it would be death to see all disputed questions
settled. The masters, one of whom at the outset said he would go
to any lengths 'rather than be dragooned by any committee of

workmen', withdrew their ban on unionism and offered to meet the men. Their terms were the old rates with some reductions, and at first the men were persuaded to resist. Early in November, however, one employer took on seventy men. Within two days came a general return to work.

The strike had snowballed along for five months. About £40,000 had been lost in wages and 1,200 combers remained out of work. Local industry had been seriously harmed: woolpack selling prices fell by about seventeen per cent. During a winter of severe distress a relief committee had to distribute oatmeal and flour weekly to hundreds of Bradford families; some of the 'aristocrats of labour' were employed to clean out the filth of Bradford beck. In the following year more power looms were installed and the attendant riots were suppressed by police and yeomanry. The employers' case was that without such machinery British industry could not continue to hold her markets in face of European competition. Yet the knowledge that trade is at their mercy seldom blunts strikers' weapons.

Strikes, whatever their kinds and causes, can in general be called 'exercises by the workers of the freedom to choose their work', its conditions and rewards. Strike occasions may be as simple as the first of the one-man strikes—that of a railway engine driver, in 1912, concerning human rights (in this case the right to get drunk while off duty) which brought out 6,000 railwaymen of the North Eastern Railway—or as complex as the strike to end all such 'sympathetic' strikes, the General Strike of 1926. Threatened then with wage reductions and longer hours— although owners' profits were not to be reduced—the miners appealed to the TUC General Council. After breakdown of negotiations, a conference of the union executives called for a strike of all those in essential industries, docks, railways, road transport, iron, steel, chemicals, printing, building, electricity and gas, in support of the miners. This challenge to the State's authority was met by emergency measures prepared beforehand —a 'Secret Organisation for the Maintenance of Supplies' and within nine days the strike was called off, by the TUC. The miners, after staying out another six months, were compelled by poverty and hunger to accept longer hours and lower wages. Many workmen were given worse jobs, lost part of their pension rights or had to leave their unions and subsequently an Act was passed declaring general strikes illegal.

All strikes, 'sit-down', 'stay-down', 'stay-in', 'lightning', 'go-slow', 'token', 'protest', 'wild-cat', 'running-sore' (as when in 1870 Fifeshire miners regularly ceased work at the end of eight hours in their struggle for a shorter working day), or 'bumper' (as in the 1820s when Barnsley linen weavers planned to call out workers factory by factory, with contributions for those on strike made by those still at work), all strikes act as the worker's weapons to redress the balance of inequality implicit in his relations with an employer. General strikes always fail since 'Lazarus dies of starvation before Dives misses a meal' (G. B. Shaw); herein lies the imbalance. The worker's need for money is greater than the employer's need for his individual services. And whilst the work-man can do nothing to change the terms of employment without the employer's consent, the reverse, for workmen under contract, would be far from true.

To 'strike work', as one strikes a sail or a mast, when stopping work at sea, came into use in its current meaning at the beginning of the Industrial Revolution. The local variant term, in Durham and Northumberland, was to 'stick'. At first a 'strike', with its suggested overtones of violence and implied revolt against the sacred doctrine of *laissez faire*, was regarded as a conspiracy against the laws of both man and God. When Durham miners went on strike, in 1844, a minister and member of a royalty-owning family wrote: 'You are resisting not the oppression of your employers, but the Will of your Maker—the ordinance of that God Who has said that in the sweat of his face shall man eat bread and Who has attached this penalty to the refusal to labour, namely, that if a man do no work neither shall he eat.' In the novel *Scarsdale*, set on the Lancashire and Yorkshire border in the 1830s, arguments for the use of machinery in weaving, put in the mouth of the mill-owner's son, are divinely supported.

> Up starveling! seize the baker's store,
> The mansion rifle, storm the mill;

> Let ironweavers steal no more
> Thy work and bid thy loom be still

cries the Lancashire striker. To him Sir Guy's son explains the need to produce cloth more cheaply to compete with foreign labour and thus to enable England to buy abroad in exchange. So it behoves them to use coal and iron and the factory machines —God's way.

Northern workmen did not react submissively. The incidence of strikes, examined industry by industry, shows that coal-miners and textile workers have had a marked proneness to strike compared with other workers well into this century. If examined region by region the incidence of strikes in these industries has also been marked in Lancashire, Cheshire, the West Riding, and to a lesser extent Northumberland and Durham. The statistics should occasion no surprise in view of the preponderance of the industries themselves in those areas—Lancashire and cotton were almost synonymous—and in the light of revealed conditions and the effects of trade fluctuations. Even so, compared with strikes in other areas such as South Wales they point to persistence of ideals or to despair, rather than to some degree of temper and pig-headedness.

In the decade following the repeal of the Combination Act, strike action came to be seen as a weapon by which trades unions could secure revolutionary change in working conditions—such as an eight-hour day—if generally enforced. In Robert Owen's view the trades unions formed into the Grand National Consolidated Trades Union, 1834, could themselves carry revolution into effect, by taking over the means of production, abolishing capitalism and so transferring the whole government of the country from master to servant. The vision of Owen and of John Doherty, founder of the Grand General Union of Operative Spinners, which spread from Lancashire and Cheshire to Yorkshire and the Midlands, expressed the impassioned hopes of a million discontented workers imprisoned by the system.

Counterblow to such dream states came from an unexpected quarter. General trade unions had taken over from their predecessors prior to 1824, when organisation could only be maintained by stealth, the practice of administering an oath to members. An obsolescent prohibition against this, made at the time of the Nore naval mutiny, existed in law. So when some Dorset farm labourers, after consultation with the GNCTU, formed a friendly society to resist wage reductions and administered the oath to members, six of the leaders were arrested, tried and in spite of massive protests given sentences of seven years transportation. The shock and example of these Tolpuddle Martyrs damped down the whole trades-union movement, as the Government intended that it should.

Employers found another countermeasure to strikers or would-be strikers—the 'document'. This device, similar to the choice of rejecting their union or receiving dismissal, as presented to operatives in the classic Bradford strike, was first used by Liverpool building employers irritated by the attitude of the increasingly powerful general trade union of builders. Before any man applied for work he must be prepared to sign a formal renunciation of his membership. Strikes followed in Liverpool and in Manchester : there were large-scale stoppages of work in Derby and Leeds, but the Builders' Union had to accept defeat. The scale of these disputes was too great for levies to yield enough to support the strikers. To many members of the GNCTU, increase of wages or shorter hours were of more immediate importance than the ultimate transformation of society, and within a year this great union, inspired by the father of English socialism, was virtually extinct.

❦

A document which three strike leaders were required to sign after defeat of a strike in Darlington in 1867, before being reinstated :

DECLARATION

We hereby promise and agree that in consideration of our being again received into the employment of Messrs. Richardson and Co. we will not, so long as we remain in their employ or in the town or neighbourhood of DARLINGTON, take any part whatsoever in commencing, carrying on, or encouraging any movement for obtaining any alteration of wages, time or rules for the workmen as a body, or for any other workmen, than

each one of us for himself; and that in case of a strike taking
place or being likely to take place, we will continue to work
as before.

First Report of the Commissioners on the Organisation and Rules of
Trade Unions, 1867

Another means of breaking strikes, resorted to by some Northern
employers, was to bring in Irish labour at low wages. It was
effective both in silk manufacturing areas and among cotton
spinners at Preston : but the employers found this weapon two-
edged, since Irish workers were notably unruly, quick to take
offence or to make unreasonable demands which they backed up
by bad language or by 'turning out' themselves. Throughout the
nineteenth century employers tried all means to break the trade-
union movement, seeing it as a curb to output and spur to rising
costs as well as an attempt to usurp their own function as managers. Cobden considered the unions to be 'founded on principles
of brutal tyranny and monopoly'. In 1851 Manchester engineers
pressed for the abolition of overtime and piecework, factors which
created unemployment : the employers formed a Central Association of Employers of Operative Engineers and then imposed a
lock-out on some 11,000 workmen. For four months the association did its best to overthrow the combination of workmen.
Although not successful in the long run it brought the union down
temporarily to a membership of only 2,000 and its funds almost
to nil.[1]

Dickens, ever intent on keeping humanity human and critical
of those who thought only in figures and averages—'representatives of the wickedest and most enormous vice of our time'—
travelled North to see for himself what a strike was like. At the
time, 1854, Preston had had a lock-out for twenty-three weeks.
He found the place 'nasty', although it was supposed to be a
model town, and the streets empty, people moping indoors. Owing

[1] The Amalgamated Society of Engineers, founded 1851, consisting of
skilled men, the key technicians of the industrial age, had a high subscription of 1s a week, a full-time paid secretary, and a considerable series of
'benefits', and tried to make unions a normal and respectable part of
society, accepting the inevitability of having two distinct groups, employers
and employed.

to cold furnaces the skies were clear. When he attended a meeting of delegates he was struck by their fortitude, good sense and restraint. After seeing the distribution of strike pay he heard a whole open-air meeting sing :

> Awake, ye sons of toil ! nor sleep
> While millions starve, while millions weep
> Demand your rights; let tyrants see
> You are resolved that you'll be free.

He came away with the certainty that capitalists might make their fortunes in such places, but that they did not make the fortunes of their employees.

After this generation of strike and counter-measure, unions entered a phase of seeking to make terms with employers rather than replace them, to operate the law and economic system to their betterment rather than to contest it, and to build up strength through organisation of the skilled trades, like the ASE, rather than to squander it in strikes. As a means of raising wages, for instance, instead of striking, unions reduced the supply of labour, by limiting apprenticeships, banning overtime and providing emigration funds for unemployed members to transfer their labour abroad. When employers fell into the trap of declaring a general lock-out to deal with some minor dispute, Sheffield union delegates announced their support for conciliation and arbitration, and set up the United Kingdom Alliance of Organised Trades. Two years later, 1868, Manchester Trades Council convened a delegate conference which was to perpetuate itself annually as the TUC. Miners and cotton workers now sought to establish a nine-hour day by legislation, instead of 'turning out', and arbitration boards were established where employers' and union representatives met round the table. Among the rank and file, voices were raised against a tendency to relate wages to selling prices, instead of pressing for minimum standards of living for workers; but when, in 1875, their pressure led to the passing of the Employers and Workmen Act—making the two sides of industry equal parties to a civil contract—it was clear that amalgamated unions had achieved a major success.

That the French, before the Commune, could refer to the tame attitude of the English 'intelligent mechanic' did not imply that 'advantage-striker' was a phrase henceforward confined in England to tennis. The artisan worker, in spite of his union, was still the victim of alternate slump and boom; but the labourer and semi-skilled worker, largely unorganised, were vastly worse off and in the Great Depression of the 80s often near to destitution. For them new unions with strong socialist backing were built up on the power to organise strikes and to pay dispute benefits. The success of the gas-workers' and general labourers' union in obtaining an eight-hour day, the great dock strike of 1889—for a 'tanner' an hour—and the London match-girls' strike, evoked much publicity and sympathy and brought to the fore socialists of the calibre of John Burns, Tom Mann and Ben Tillett. General labourers' unions with low rates of contribution spread rapidly from one industry to another. There was revival of the theory of strike action to prepare for a general strike on a national scale, which would lead to social and industrial revolution. Since it was clear that trade-union freedom and the unrestricted play of economic forces could not provide workers with security and a fair standard of living, industry therefore should be owned by the State but controlled by the workers employed in it. A practical result was the formation of the National Union of Railwaymen by amalgamation of the three chief railway unions.

Soon after the turn of the century an important stage was reached in attempts to secure national administration of industry by the other means, constitutional action ('We'll take to making the laws, O'). In the 1906 General Election twenty-nine candidates of the Labour Representation Committee (secretary Ramsay Macdonald), which was to become the Labour Party, were returned together with thirteen miner candidates. (BRADFORD was the formative centre of the ILP.) Yet disputes and strikes again mounted in intensity and violence. For workers in many industries real wages were not as good after 1900 as they had been before and the successful example of the dockers was still fresh in mind. Great waves of strikes involving mainly miners, railwaymen and dockers resulted in alarming loss of working days—over

40,000,000 in the year 1912 alone. (For comparison an average
of 7,560,000 days were lost annually in the period 1922-32, excluding the General Strike year's 102,000,000.) Hull, Manchester,
Liverpool witnessed clashes between strikers and soldiers or police.
The struggle for control of industry, after the manner of the
French syndicates, led to further combination until finally railwaymen, miners and transport workers formed a triple alliance,
pledged to negotiate together and to support each other by strike
action as necessary.

Among such general manifestations of discontent with the
system and the conditions of labour some Northern industries
maintained a fair record of forbearance and arbitration. Durham
mines saw the first standing joint committee of owners and men,
Northumberland the first proper conciliation board. The miners'
unions survived the great depression of the 80s and opposed the
idea of a national strike on the question of a 'living wage'.[1] There
was considerable action against the three-shift system in 1908,
but again in the immediately post-war strike wave, miners' ballots
showed an anti-strike feeling in Durham. Native caution,
relatively good housing—from which strikers knew that they
could be evicted and their goods dumped in the road—together
with locally strong Nonconformist influence and employers'
appreciation of union attitudes all helped towards moderation.
Even during the depression of the 1930s and the prolonged
miseries when Jarrow's shipbuilding was killed, Durham workers
displayed an unusual degree of forbearance.

◆◆◆

Though always anti-violence—'strikes among working men
are like wars among nations, bad things at best'—Non-con-
formist opinion on the subject of a living wage was forceful :
'It is what the miners say they by the endurance of cold and
want have been contending for; a remuneration for their toil
upon which they can maintain themselves and their families
with decency and comfort. And who ought to labour for less
than this? There may be some difficulty in solving what con-

---

[1] The contemporary situation was dramatically handled by G. A. Henty in
Facing Death—or the Hero of Vaughan Pit.

stitutes a living wage : but one thing is certain that manufacturers and coal-owners cannot in the interests of social wellbeing be allowed much longer to compete and undersell one
another in securing contracts by lowering the wages of the
worker till life sinks to the level of a bare existence. It is one of
the primary rights of man not simply to exist, but to have the
chance to live as a rational being. . . . Low prices are not
caused by the workers, but by employers competing with one
another for the contracts of associated monopolists like railway,
gas and other companies. The rule that prices should govern
wages is a vicious rule.   Primitive Methodist Magazine, 1893

The Wesleyan Methodists were apolitical and keen not to offend
the middle class.

~~~

Like miners, textile workers, especially those in cotton, tend
to live in the close community of their own 'cotton' towns or
'wool' towns with little access until recently to alternative employment in times of depression and with a strong sense of solidarity.
The number of married women employed ties workers to the
district of their homes. While workshop problems alone seldom
led to strikes of the smaller type, textile strikes, mainly in the cotton
towns, when called on basic issues thus involved a high proportion of workers. The strikes arose out of demands for wage increases, claims for unemployment pay for time lost by reduction
of hours, opposition to the employment of non-union labour and
attempted wage reductions, or the complex issue of 'more looms
to a weaver'.

The lock-out of 1911-12 for instance was the first serious
struggle between employers and employed in Blackburn for a
period of twenty-eight years. It began in the Great Harwood
district by a strike of weavers who were authorised by their association to refuse to work in the same mill as one young woman who
was not a member of any trade union, and simultaneously in
Accrington by a strike against the employment of two non-
unionists, a man and his wife. There had for months, indeed
years, been a determination to make every weaver join one of the
weavers' associations, but employers declined to take any part in

compelling their workpeople to do so and resented the stoppage of their mills by strikes on such a question. They gave due notice of retaliation, and on the Wednesday after Christmas 1911 the great majority of the weaving mills in Lancashire were closed till further notice : the workpeople were locked out.

Outsiders can scarcely appreciate the intensity of feeling between the conflicting parties on occasions like this. The ethics of strikes and lock-outs, their utility or futility, do not influence either masters or men so much as the grim determination to fight to the last ditch for what they deem to be their rights. On this occasion the operatives were fighting for the dismissal of one person in Great Harwood and two persons in Accrington, but their great object was to bring into line with the majority of workers those non-members of their associations who received all the benefits which trade unionism secured for the working classes without contributing a penny to their funds.

The number of operatives locked out was about 160,000 of whom 29,000 were in Blackburn : 40,000 spinners and cardroom hands were also affected indirectly, for the spinning mills had to go on half time immediately the demand for their yarn ceased. The loss of the working people in wages was estimated at £300,000 per week, certainly not less than £1,000,000 for the period of the lock-out; the settlement came by an agreement to resume work on 22 January 1912 on the old conditions of employment.

Altogether five great strikes occurred in the period 1911-21 among cotton, jute and woollen operatives, three of them developing into lock-outs. After the post-war contraction of the export trade, accompanied by persistent short-time working in cotton and reductions of wages, further strikes brought relations between employers and operatives to eventual breakdown. Collective bargaining could handle or obviate local and district differences but it needed all the Ministry of Labour's powers of manœuvre to work out methods of conciliation for this long-suffering industry, whose operatives lived on vain hopes for a recovery and improvements that never came.

In time of war industrial peace prevails; one great need overrules all others. Controls, compulsory arbitration and suspension of many trade union rules and practices in the First World War formed a guarantee against almost all union-supported strikes. There were big strikes at Barrow-in-Furness (as well as those of women workers in cotton, munitions, transport and electrical engineering), not in pursuance of trade disputes, but as an attempt to change Government policy in the prosecution of the war and these were dealt with under the Defence of the Realm and Military Service Acts. Strikers could be conscripted into the forces unless they resumed work.

◌◟ᴡᴡᴡ◞◌

Women, perhaps because of their lack of economic opportunity and responsibility, have not been backward in strike action or in supporting men's strikes. In the first World War women cotton workers, munition, engineering and transport workers engaged in strikes at LEEDS, BARROW, BRADFORD, RAWTENSTALL, LIVERPOOL : women militantly supported the 40-hour week movement of ship-builders in 1919. They were conspicuous in the great textile strikes of 1922 and the depression years. (According to a survey in 1937 the proportion of married women in cotton was 52 per cent compared with 29 per cent for all industries.)

It is only when workers have some degree of cohesion that unrest takes the form of strikes : with young women in, say, the clothing industry it may appear instead in a high rate of labour turnover.

Strikes, K. C. J. C. Knowles

Women also undertook some of the less-publicised 'dirty jobs' like the 'pit-brow lasses' of WIGAN who helped to keep the home fires burning in and after 1914.

◌◟ᴀᴀ◞◌

In the Second World War dilution of labour, direction of employment and the National Arbitration Act were again accepted by the unions. There were many short, small strikes—mainly in mining—but the actual loss of working time by strike action was less than half of that in the First War. With trades unions ever more closely associated with the State and Ernest

Bevin, Secretary of the TGWU for twenty years, as Minister of
Labour fewer mistakes were made in the handling of disputes.

From the time of the First War a figure of considerable influence
in the industrial field of action emerged—the elected spokesman
for his fellows at their place of work, the shop steward. The
engineering industry had had shop stewards since 1878, but it
was the workshop problems and reaction against the wartime
emergency restrictions which gave the steward his power and
recognition. Shop stewards, handling the interpretation of wage
agreements or negotiation of piece rates on the spot, are in a
strong position compared with the TU branch official perhaps
employed elsewhere : management tends to consult them inform-
ally rather than the full-time officers. Their militancy, compared
with that of their unions (especially in the 'restraint' period after
the Second World War), has also spotlighted their function. In
combination, or at a time of unofficial stoppages, or 'inspired' by
political motives, shop stewards have maintained a position that
tests both their own and management's nerves.

ᏩᏬ

The Ideal Union

The union is my shepherd, I shall not work.
It maketh me to lie down on the job; it leadeth me beside the
still factories.
It restoreth my insurance benefit.
Yea, though I walk through the valley of the shadow of unemployment I will fear no recrimination, for the union is with
me; its restrictive practices and shop stewards they comfort me.
It prepareth a works committee before me in the presence of
my employers; it anointeth my hand with pay rises, and my
bank balance runneth over.
Surely work bonuses and union control shall follow me all the
days of my life, and I shall dwell in a council house for ever.

Parody of the 23rd psalm, from a parish magazine

ᏩᏬ

'To obtain a blessing on its labours (combination) must work
under the direction of a high and intelligent will : incapable of

I

being misled by passion or excitement' (Mrs Gaskell). Passion and excitement are factors seldom conspicuously absent from strike action : a high and intelligent will is conspicuously present only exceptionally in the strategy or political motivation. 'Rag-outs' they call miners' strikes of lost temper in Yorkshire, when men put on their coats and leave the pit if anything goes wrong. It has not failed to attract notice that the famous 'tanner' strike of 1889 started one blazing hot August day with a trivial dispute which suddenly spread from dock to dock : that wide-spreading strikes and August temperatures of 97° F coincided in 1911, and that in an average year the main striking peaks occur in May and August. Hot tempers and hot weather to enjoy 'playing'? The cynic will quote *Strike Pay* in which D. H. Lawrence makes a woman call the strike 'gala-time' for miners. 'That's all men strike for, indeed. They enjoy themselves, they do that. Ripping and racing and drinking from morn till night. So long as they get something to eat at home what more do they want?' The fact remains that workers can better maintain strikes in favourable summer weather than in the crippling conditions of winter.

───※───

One day my father did not go to work, nor did any other miner. Adults talked of a strike. As the days lengthened into weeks men squatting on their haunches in the alleys and at street corners talked of their need of food for their children, of their desire for money to clothe themselves and their families, and spoke of ways of obtaining fuel to cook the food they had. To see that the bairns had enough to eat blossomed into a social concern, and if the community did not always succeed, the fault could not be laid at the door of the tradesmen of the town. Then small shopkeepers gave credit not merely till it hurt but till it crippled them. Some closed down; others went bank-rupt; all were owed more than they were ever likely to recover. One, the owner of a fish-and-chip shop, gave several free meals to the youngsters in the neighbourhood. We sat down at long benches in a back-yard and devoured quantities of boiled cod, potatoes and butter beans.

Many of the miners acquired fishing lines and invaded the harbour pier to catch at least one meal a day. The pier was,

I believe, forbidden territory in those days. Certainly I have no recollection of any fishing taking place there prior to the strike, but now the men were in an ugly mood and they were left to do their fishing unmolested.

Periodically we received strike pay, and loaves of bread were also provided by the Union. These were distributed once a week at the Miners' Hall.

Pit-Yacker, George Hitchin, 1962

❧

Small, apparently frivolous strikes do happen—or severe strikes for apparently frivolous reasons, such as a complaint about a vindictive foreman, and 'taking a holiday' as the Sheffield journeymen and Nottingham knitters used to do, are words lightly used for some strike actions, but the root causes for strikes are neither light nor frivolous.

On a sunny midsummer day, a hundred years ago, Coketown 'seemed to be frying in oil—the mills baked at a fierce heat —the atmosphere was like the breath of the simoon'. Since then physical conditions in workshop and factory have improved immeasurably, and workers are ready to lay down tools if the inside temperature rises unduly. There is still, of course, 'the factory smell of oil-suds, machinery and shaved steel that surrounded you with an air in which pimples grew and prospered on your face and shoulders' (Alan Sillitoe); but it is the whole character of industrial work which leads to the sparking-off of strikes.

Not only hours and wages, but the complete syndrome of carrying on a lifetime's fatiguing, monotonous, frustrating, often unhealthy work, usually for the private profit of others and certainly to the detriment or drying up of their own creative impulses and intelligent responses, underlies such explosions of unrest. The management's criterion of output rate and profitability, the closely supervised 'time-and-motion' standards of working, cramp the soul. A fully automatic weaving shed, a centrimist automatic air-conditioning plant, some managements' watered-down version of the Whitley Committee's recommendations—informal conferences with foremen and supervisors on two or three Saturday mornings in the year 'with coffee and cigarettes and everyone chats'—are not the real answer.

'Many people want to work for more than just wages', says an enlightened West Riding textile manufacturer : 'they want satisfaction too; a sense of doing something worth while, of creating something useful or beautiful, they want to put something of themselves in their work'. An industrial psychologist finds that jobs with few responsibilities, a dependent 'do this, do that' relationship to a supervisor and uncreative work, all produce regressive behaviour and aggressive modes of expressing it—ie strikes. In industry only directors, managers and craftsmen enjoy creative activity; the worker who is most likely to be contented is the responsible craftsman with some degree of independence— a type increasingly thin on the ground. What was lost a hundred and fifty years ago in removing the craftsman from the centre of the industrial scene in the name of competitive enterprise cannot now be replaced.

After the economic crisis of 1931 (and the stubborn defensive strikes in cotton and wool against wage decreases or 'more looms to the weaver') industry enjoyed a period of seven years without any large-scale strike—that is one involving a hundred thousand or more workers. It might have been thought that the strike weapon was to be sheathed. In fact under new conditions of negotiating machinery and union controls, strikes, instead of looming long and large, have flickered short and sharply, as token or lightning demonstrations, with maximum nuisance value. Whereas in the period 1922-32 a total of 7,560,000 working days were lost annually compared to the average annual loss of 1,920,000 days in 1934-54, within the latter period the number of strikes increased from under 1,000 to nearly 2,000 per year. Hours of work and wages—often pushed up nowadays by 'peaceful' methods—give place to the more general 'working arrangements', including rules and discipline, as their discoverable causes. Wage structure has almost come full circle, back to the early eighteenth-century position where State takes control, hand-in-hand now with the TUC. But 'though no strong cause for open belligerence existed as in the bad days talked about, it persisted for more subtle reasons

that could hardly be understood but were nevertheless felt'. Sillitoe's comment on the relations between workman and foreman
applies equally to man and machine system.

∽∾∽

The Government and the Trades Union Congress have
established confidential consultative procedures to further each
other's incomes policy. These have already progressed to a stage
at which the Department of Economic Affairs has tacitly agreed
to accept TUC recommendations on references to the Prices
and Incomes Board.

The extent of the TUC wage vetting committee's success is
a direct corollary of its ability to persuade unions, whose claims
exceed the various criteria of incomes policy, to pare the claims
down until they do conform. The transaction is of a private
family nature, from which intruders are excluded.

The National Union of Dyers, Bleachers and Textile Workers
is a Bradford-based textile union with a membership of 120,000
in the industry whose general secretary—a Yorkshireman in his
mid-forties named Jack Peel—joined the vetting committee in
his first year on the General Council.

Early this year the union submitted a claim to the TUC for
vetting. It amounted to an increase for the union's members,
whose average earnings are £18 a week, of 5½ per cent. There
was a demand for a straight wage increase across the board of
3½ per cent, half an hour off the working week, and two more
days paid holiday.

Plainly, the claim did not conform. Although there were
lower paid workers in the industry earning less than £14 a
week, the union did not have enough information about the
structure of the industry to isolate them, and tailor the claim
to push up their wages at the expense of the higher paid men.

Peel was told by his colleagues on the committee that he did
not have any chance of getting the claim through the Government's net unless it was pared down. Peel, who had first hand
experience of what the Government was likely to accept,
agreed. When the claim was presented to the textile employers,
the union asked for a 3 per cent wage increase, and one extra
day's holiday. The employers accepted, and agreed to an
operative date of May 1.

Sunday Times, June 1967

∽∾∽

Friction still causes strike. 'Outside the factory sticks were wielded, bricks thrown and a senior Stockport police officer had his arm broken' reads the report (26 August 1967) of a protracted engineering firm dispute, in which the management's refusal to deal with shop stewards hampered negotiation to settle a strike that began when women were employed on what the unions claimed was men's work and led to dismissals and mass picketing. A strike's activating surface is less likely now to be the 'living wage' in the nineteenth-century sense than 'human rights', sometimes of a trivial, actually of a far broader kind. Significantly the latest Labour Party pamphlet on *Industrial Democracy* does not press the claim to put workers' representatives on the boardrooms of private industry, but to extend TU prerogatives into negotiations on such things as safety, redundancy, dismissals and the implications of mergers. Industrial bloody-mindedness can sometimes be a man who half remembers what yesterday's bosses did to his father.

SHOP

Before the Second World War almost any child in a northern
town might be sent three or four times a week to the 'Corp'—
the local branch of the Co-operative Wholesale Society. In
HALIFAX it was painted green and orange, like the local buses.
There were large display windows on either side of the door, at
which no one ever stopped to look since all the 'goods' seemed
to be either dummy packets of oatmeal or soap powders. The
door opened with a 'ping' from an invisibly placed bell and one's
nostrils were instantly assailed by a mingled aroma of Pelaw
polish, firelighters, sawdust and slightly 'off' fat.

Inside the floor boards were uneven, hollowed by the tread of
many shoppers and by the iron wheels of the trolleys that took
sacks and barrels from the door to dark recesses behind the
counter. This, a solid wooden construction, rubbed to a chestnut
glow by many hands, bags and babies' bottoms, extended right
across the shop. It was separated into sections by geometric stacks
of tins of peaches, pots of jam, packets of ground rice or flour.
Behind the counter rose tiers of wooden drawers, going up into
the arches of a blackened, cobwebbed roof : some had labels,
cinnamon, nutmeg, cloves, ginger, mixed spice.

In these sections the customer had a sense of privacy in pur-
chasing and consultation with the shopman. A dim, naked electric
light bulb provided illumination both day and night, the shop

167

windows being blocked by dark wooden partitions. Strings strung across the shop held floppy oat cakes; sacks of potatoes, apples, of sad-looking cabbage and oranges stood around the floor; sides of bacon hung from hooks in the ceiling to be reached down by a long pole; butter arrived in barrels from which slabs were cut and moulded to shape by an assistant dexterously wielding two wooden butter pats. Silver Seal margarine was much in evidence and the assistants had soiled white coats and bluish-red hands.

Next to the corner shop and the market, the Co-op is the most characteristic feature of traditional shopping habits in the industrial North. The co-operative retail business was begun at ROCHDALE in 1844. A shop was then rented for £10 a year, twenty-eight people contributed £1 each as capital, and stock at first was confined to five commodities in general use—butter, sugar, flour, oatmeal and candles. There was to be no giving of credit, only cash purchases, no cutting of prices in competition with the 'shop at the corner'. The capital was to be paid for at five per cent and the surplus on trading (or profit) was to be shared as dividend among members in proportion to their custom. Members had votes in the affairs of the society in proportion to the shares that they held. 'Divvy', if uncashed, was credited to capital and so formed a means of painless saving for working people. Strictly cash accounts meant that the society saved on book-keeping costs and avoided bad debts.

The Co-operative idea spread over most districts of the North, especially the industrial areas of Lancashire and Yorkshire and also of the north Midlands, where factory towns had not the same service amenities as older established towns. In 1864 the Co-operative Wholesale Society was founded in MANCHESTER, with capital provided by the retail societies, which obtained a dividend on purchases in exactly the same way as customers did from their local shop. The societies in Lancashire, Yorkshire and the Midlands benefited from this direct means of supply and the further margin of profit-sharing, although CWS goods were not pushed at the expense of other brands, but only when the customer expressed no preference. 'Fashion goods' naturally took second place to standardised commodities.

Co-ops have flourished ever since, greatly expanding both in membership and in range of trade. When BURNLEY celebrated the centenary of its society in 1960, it had progressed from the days when members of the committee served behind the counter of its only shop for three hours each evening to the present employment of 370 staff for 49 grocery shops, 9 butchers, 2 department stores, mobile shop and market stall. Coal, coke and milk supply, banking, funerals and a travel agency form part of its services. The society in ROCHDALE built and owns many of that town's terrace houses. 'It pays to come Co-operative shopping'— as the match-box labels say.

WORKINGTON
BEEHIVE CO-OPERATIVE Tel 3581
THESE MODERN DEPARTMENTS ARE AT YOUR SERVICE
Drapery – Tailoring – Boots
Furnishing – Electrix – Hardware
Grocery and Provisions
Fruit – Milk – Café and Catering
Coal Delivery
Confectionery from our own Bakery

Free Delivery of Goods
Free insurance on purchases
Full dividend on all purchases
Easy hire purchase facilities
FUNERALS
FURNISHED COMPLETE

Altogether by the end of the nineteenth century there were 1,439 societies with over 1,700,000 members. In 1932 the number of societies had been reduced by amalgamation to 1,171 but the total of members exceeded 6,700,000. Many changes have taken place, of course. Even BURNLEY's society admits that the department selling clogs has closed—but it still sells the traditional shawls of Lancashire. To the Northern child remembering t'Co-op number—to ensure the divvy on goods bought—is still a required duty; the divvy may be as much as 3s in the pound. And as he or she grows up, having a suit or coat *not* bought at the Co-op is a cherished landmark, because it can then be in the fashion, instead of a year behind or in 'good, sound' style.

Markets have meant much to the Northern housewife in her concern that every penny in the family purse should obtain its full value. Their origin in the Middle Ages, when the surplus of corn, wool and animal products in the country would be sold for the specialised products of town craftsmen can still be seen. Then goods were brought into the churchyard for protection against thieves, or, when the town had in its charter a right to hold a market—BRADFORD, for example, like WIGAN, was granted a charter for a market by Henry III in the thirteenth century and it was first held near the parish church—stalls for fruit and vege-tables were set up on a fixed day each week in certain streets. Very often the same streets, not always near the church, see a weekly spread of stalls today : if traders are there by ancient right the local authority has no power to prevent the holding of such street markets, but market halls have often been built or rebuilt on the original site.

◦◦◦

As far back as the year 1272 Almondbury (HUDDERSFIELD) boasted a weekly market. When this market was discontinued is not known, but it was probably in the year 1672 when powers were granted to the Ramsden family to hold a market in Huddersfield. The Huddersfield markets were formerly held in the open air in the old market place, New Street, and also on the site of the present Market Hall in King Street, which was then called the Shambles.

In 1857 the then Local Authority—the Improvement Commissioners—took the Market tolls on lease. Subsequently in 1876 the Corporation purchased from Sir John Ramsden all the market rights and tolls. The foundation stone of the present Market Hall which was built on the so-called Shambles was laid in 1878.

The Market Hall is built in the Decorated Gothic through-out, a typical specimen of the Gothic revival, and presents an elegant appearance, especially as far as the main front is con-cerned. The market comprises 56 shops and 166 stalls : there

are on the upper and lower side of the building—that is outside—shops for butchers etc. On each side of the entrances are
shops for fishmongers and other trades. Glazed awnings protect the shops facing the streets.

Huddersfield Official Handbook, 1954

Carved shields at the entrances to the market bear the arms of
Charles II, who gave a charter to Mr John Ramsden to hold a
market on the site on which the Market Hall stands, and of Queen
Victoria in whose reign the hall was erected.

⤜⤛

For supplies that were not produced locally and were bought
irregularly fairs were held from the Middle Ages onwards with
a particular street for each class of goods. The fairs also had their
independence; they were subject not to the manorial courts but
to their own 'Piepowder' court,[1] for settling disputes between
buyer and seller. Cloth, local or foreign, raw wool, hides, silk,
spices were their commodities and they continued in popularity
up to the nineteenth century when rail distribution made them
largely unnecessary. The British Industries Fair is one of their
descendants and the amusement fair, the traditional aftermath of
mediaeval business, their regular reminder. In HUDDERSFIELD the
Markets & Fairs committee has control of the pleasure fairs held
at Easter and September; in DERBY, whose right to hold fairs was
incorporated in the markets charter given by King John, pleasure
fairs take place every Easter and August.

Northern towns are proud of their market tradition. The newcomer to LEEDS or DONCASTER, BURY or NEWCASTLE will be impressed by their size, range and popularity, whether held in the
vast covered halls with regular well-stocked stalls, or in the open,
as at BARNSLEY, STOCKTON, SHEFFIELD and DARLINGTON, as sup-
plementary markets for mixed goods and cheaper lines. Celia
Fiennes notes, in her description of CHESTERFIELD (1698), that
'the Church stands in a place of eminency, the town looks well,
the streets good, the market very large . . . like some little fair.'
Twenty-five years later Defoe remarks on this 'handsome, popu-
lous town, well-built and well-inhabited with a very good market

---

[1] Piepowder = *pieds poudreux*, from the dusty feet of travelling merchants.

well-stored with provisions'. CHESTERFIELD'S present market hall, market place of covered stalls and the old Shambles near the church—with a Tudor pub and street names such as Knifesmithgate, Packers' Row, Saltergate and Beetwell Street nearby—retain their importance in the town's centre. Market day in such places is the time when everyone and everything feels more alive.

The outsider who aims to get to the hub of life in an old industrial town should go round the market, preferably on Saturday. The bustle, the backchat, the bargaining, the throw-away offers on china stall or in dress stuffs, stockings or cutlery, especially at the approach of the Christmas season, the elbowing, bag and basket-laden good-humoured crowd, the notices—*Beware of Pickpockets*, the tea-bars with their local specialities, crumpets, pikelets, lardy-cakes, Eccles cakes, buttered toast 6d, ham sandwich 10d, the bright lights and warm air from the floor gratings, the sense of a spree even if spending here is itself an economy—all make a cheerful haven amid the murk and drizzle of a BURSLEM or a BURNLEY winter's day. In BURNLEY, whose market charter dates from 1294, traders bring piles of fleecy sheets, candlewick blankets, bedspreads, rugs direct from the mill, to sell at rock-bottom prices; some weeks a whole alley is devoted to 'special lines' of pots and china, at other times to skirt-lengths and silks. In the provision market one jostles between stalls of trotters, steaming black pudding, Lancashire 'tasty' cheese, liquorice root (among the herbal remedies), havercake, pots of 'mums and crisp fresh-cut lettuces. A good many of the vegetable stalls are run by market gardeners who bring in their own green stuff.

STOCKTON open-air market, an almost impassable mile of double-banked stalls ranged down the middle of the High Street, is the Mecca of shoppers for miles around. Anything from garter elastic to 'Gaieties of Paris' playing cards, garden plants to gas-pokers and gorgonzola cheese, can be found if one's elbows are active enough to get past the live tortoises and Jews' patter, pudding basins and cockle stalls.

In most markets the real bargains in food are to be had late on Saturdays. The housewives with the slenderest purses come here, the old-age pensioners and the night-shift Pakistanis, to get the scraping of the barrel of potatoes, the remaining bruised apples, the last few damaged tomatoes, loose bananas or wilting greens at 'give-away' prices. The butcher hands out a few bits of left-over meat with a pound of dripping and any old bones that he does not want; the fishmonger offers something extra 'for the cat'. In hard times all market stalls are carefully compared before anything is bought. In the worst of times, the old-clothes sections of such markets as DONCASTER or NEWCASTLE see much 'picking over'. (Newcastle, in addition to the glass-roofed Grainger Market, the Fish Market and the Green Market, has a fourth Saturday Market, by the quayside dealing solely in second-hand goods—though it is not so organised as the second-hand clothes market of GLASGOW Green, where most of that city's nineteenth-century working-class were clad.) To the onlooker, indoor markets with their lights and vendors' cries and bright displays of goods, or outside stalls with their pyramids of fruit, vegetables and flowers lit by pressure lamp or naphtha flare, are oases of enjoyment in a bleak milieu. To the poorer class, staggering home with heavy string bags after much standing and shoving, they are lifeblood. The loss of old open markets is nearly always regretted. 'Aye, t'new market's all covered in, so stall rent is higher,' said a market car-park attendant, 'and prices is higher too, see.'

ᐠᐯᐯᐠ

BOILED-BOOT SHOPS

The question of boots, both for children and grown-up people, is with the badly-off a constant difficulty, and one of the most serious that they have to face; and the miserable foot-gear of the women and children especially—the men are obliged to have more or less good boots to go to work in—is a constant source of discomfort and of injury to health. One reason why so many of the poor women go about with skirts which drag about in the mud is that they do not want to display what they have on their feet by holding their skirts up. A working girl said on one occasion that she thought the mark of a 'real lady' was that she wore a short skirt and neat boots, this last representing to the working-girl almost the unattainable. Boiled-boot shops are still met with (in MIDDLESBROUGH). 'Boiled' boots are old boots begged, found in the street etc.,

picked up, patched, polished and sold at a low price. There
are various old clothes shops, market stalls, hawkers' barrows,
at which men's suits as well as women's clothes can be bought
for a trifling sum.   At the Works, Lady Bell, 1907

Lady Bell, daughter-in-law of Sir Lowthian Bell, FRS, iron-
master and colliery owner, Co Durham, interested herself in the
daily lives of workmen engaged in the iron trade, 'huge measuring
gauge of the national prosperity', and tried 'to put a piece of that
prosperity under the microscope' in one of its centres of greatest
activity.

Apart from the idiosyncrasies of Northern manners manifest in
swop shops (motto 'we buy owt') and t'cobblers shop (male gossip
exchange), tally shops (where only traders' tokens or tickets can be
used) and tommy shops (whose abuses were partly offset by the
fact that payment in goods at least meant wages spent on the
family), cut-price shops and the old hush shops (unlicensed beer
shops common in Manchester area a century ago), there are two
further types of shop, often mutually supporting, which have their
place in all working-class communities—the corner shop and the
pawn shop.

> On Saturday evenings the whole working class streams from
> the slums into the main streets (and inns). When the revellers
> have no more money they go to the nearest pawnshop with what-
> ever they have. MANCHESTER has over sixty pawnshops : in
> SALFORD there are ten or twelve in Chapel Street alone (Engels).

These shops were not the supports only of drinking to excess.
John Barton, in the novel *Mary Barton*, 'went upstairs for his
better coat and his one gay red-and-yellow silk pocket-handker-
chief' before going to the pawnshop where he raised 5s. With this
he bought meat, and a loaf of bread, candles, chips (firewood) and
from a retail yard a couple of hundredweight of coal—necessaries
to help out a fellow worker, unemployed and down with typhoid
fever in the MANCHESTER of the 1840s.

'Price and Jones's pawnshop stood at one point of a triangle;
the other two points were occupied, respectively, by a church and
a palatial beerhouse, each large, commodious and convenient' in
the MANCHESTER of the 1930s (Walter Greenwood). Despite the

beerhouse's convenience the women who then come in with boots, shoes, clogs, girls' cheap, gaudy dance frocks, men's Sunday suits, mixed bundles of bedding, table linen and underclothing done up in cotton-print wrappers, and even pension books, are not waiting to buy a 'nip', but to get a shilling and then try and make it do the work of two. With the money they squeeze from Mr Price in exchange for the family wardrobe, including the lodger's best suit, they must first pay off their 'tick' account for food at the street-corner provision shop before obtaining more 'tick' for the coming week. 'Half a crown (for the ten shilling pension book) and four and six (for the suit) is seven shillings' bawls Mr Price, 'threepence for hanging the suit (instead of bundling up so that it shows tell-tale creases like a concertina) and twopence for tickets leaves six and sixpence. Thank you ma'am'. Even he values an extra penny! Pawn shops may not be as much in evidence today, but in such districts old clothes shops, junk and 'swop' shops partly fill their place.

In the general development of retailing goods the corner shop fulfils a special need. Prior to the nineteenth century certain household goods, for which there was not a very wide market, such as cutlery, cloth, cotton thread, needles, tape and ribbon, were brought to the house door by a pedlar or packman-merchant.

Parson Woodforde's *Diary*, 31 March 1784, has a detailed reference to the pedlar's wares :

Of one Bagshaw a Derbyshire Man and who carries a pack with divers things in it to sell, bought a whole piece of black Ribbon 18 yard of it at 3½d per Yard worth 5d pd 0.5.3. Nancy bought some coloured Ribbon at 5d worth 8d To a Qr of a Pound of 9d Thread worth 10d I pd. 0.2.10 To a Qr of a Pound of 4d Thread very good pd. 1.4 To 2 oz of 4d Thread and 2 oz of 3d Thread pd 1.0 Gave the Maids 2 oz each besides of 4d Thread 1.4d. Very hard frost this evening. Snow all day before.

For the products of tailor, milliner, bootmaker, in most communities their workshops served as retail shops. For those commodities not produced by the trader there were specialist shops such as the butcher's, grocer's, draper's, druggist's, fishmonger's. Formerly, in the larger towns, dealers in a particular line of goods concentrated their shops in the same street, with a characteristic name—Corn Street, Wine Street, Bread Street, Milk Street. But the new industrial suburbs and rapidly growing boom towns of the nineteenth century needed different shopping facilities—shops selling all the various commodities grouped together in the areas of dense population. In support of these tightly-knit shopping areas there was a place also for the sort of general shop that serves a country village and that could supply, like the packman, almost doorstep service in each little congerie of streets. The corner shop with its medley of lines from aspirins to anniversary cards, bath-brick to babies' comforters, cornflour to corn-plasters, dolly mixtures to dubbin is the ever-popular answer.

Many corner shops form part of a house, perhaps one room which the shop-keeper enters from his back kitchen, and in heavily built up areas there may be a shop for every street. Deeplish, a suburb of ROCHDALE with a total of 1,600 houses, has 77 shops, an average of one to each 55 people, and many of them are corner shops. Like other small retail shops for which little capital was available to start up in business, they proliferated once the railways had ensured that stocks could be replenished at regular short intervals instead of being bought in bulk annually. At their lowest level they fit into the pattern of crowded alleys and back streets blocked at the ends by mills, with their public houses, pawnbrokers', rag-and-bone warehouses and dirty provision stores, described both by Engels and Mrs Gaskell as typical of the MAN-CHESTER scene. Once the pedestrian left the broad main streets with their better-quality goods displays and shop premises—well-filled lighted windows where haunches of venison, Stilton cheeses, moulds of jelly tantalised the street urchins and the out-of-work—he was among back-street shops which sold tea and sugar in half-penny worths, because working-class women could not afford to spend more than that on one article.

In contrast to the town shopkeeper, like the druggist 'whose smooth manners seemed to have been salved over with his own

Strike: Preston strike 1854

Strike: Blackburn strike meeting 1861

Strike: Seamen out

Strike: (above) Miners' strike-pay arriving; (below) Soup queue

Strike: Law and order

Strike: (above) Public exhortation; (below) At the coal face

Strike: Still it goes on

Shop: Supply line

Shop: (above) Co-op, West Cumberland; (below) Cut-price, Thornaby-on-Tees

Shop: (above) New Market
(left) Market Day

Shop: Roundsman, Halifax

Shop: (above) Corner shop, Darlington; (below) Stockport

Shop: New style, Jarrow

School: (above) 'Ragged' class 1857

(below) Textile Lab, Leeds 1860

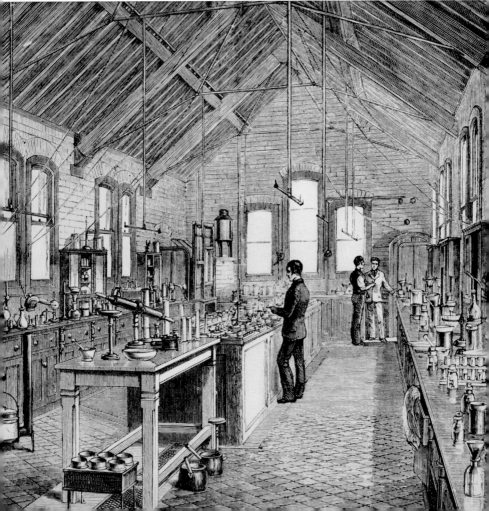

School: (above) Playtime, Workington

(right) Hometime, Burnley

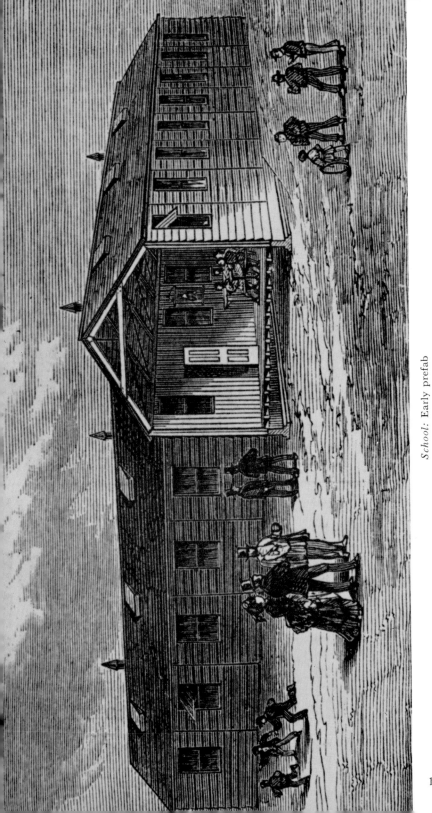

School: Early prefab

spermaceti', the corner shopkeeper was and is likely to be work-ing-class himself. He runs a one-man show, tries to stock every-thing, takes down orders, remembers individual likings, asks after the newest baby, ties up awkward parcels, tolerates children's games outside the window—an oasis of cheerfulness and light in the foggy streets, and even on Sunday is ready to serve. His shop provides one of the hubs of local life and a meeting place for housewives : among them he has to preserve the tricky balance between 'not giving credit as a rule' and allowing 'tick' during a trade depression. If he does not serve his community in its times of need he may find himself without customers. In the North East of England many of his sort found that they had to shut up shop during the worst times of depression, simply because neither their customers nor they themselves could afford to buy any longer. There are other pitfalls : the man who has saved enough to buy a small corner shop—selling cigarettes and tobacco, newspapers, sweets or groceries—as a means of escape from wage slavery, may find his slavery to the counter no less strict and his expected reward sabotaged by various trading clubs or cut-price chain stores opening in the vicinity. His trade may be taken away alto-gether when re-housing schemes uproot the neighbourhood. 'Red-hot bargains at a give-away price' in small shops usually find themselves with an ingenuous new owner trying desperately to sell superfluous wares.

ᘯᗢᕈ

My mother bought all her groceries at the little shop at the corner. I often ran down there for a jug of vinegar or half a loaf of bread or two ounces of tea at the end of the week when funds were getting low. 'You'll go further and fare worse' my mother used to say. . . . My father was all for independence and private initiative : we preferred the friendly service and superior quality of goods at the little grocer's shop. Even the Co-op came in for my father's censure. There were other, bigger shops at the top of the street, but it was the little corner shop, smelling of tea and soap and cocoa and cheese and fresh-baked bread that had the first place in our affections.

Sorrows, Passions and Alarms, James Kirkup, 1959

ᘯᗢᕈ

The shopping pattern is changing and in some northern towns
has changed almost completely since the Second World War. In
DERBY, for example—noted for its warm-hearted and colourful
indoor markets (heated in winter and cooled by fans in summer)
and its open market of 258 stalls lit by fluorescent lamps for
Friday and Saturday trade—away from the centre the supermarket, with its wire baskets, eye-catching reductions and adding
machines, is making inroads on the shopping scene. There is, of
course, a good variety of personal shops and of big department
stores (a successful shopkeeper's means of expansion by adding to
the line of goods sold to the same customer), even special fabric
shops catering for 'Clever little women good with a needle'.

When Gordon Selfridge came to London in 1906 British
retail trade was still based on the personal contact between
craftsman and customer and offered satisfaction in almost
direct proportion to the customer's means. The departmental
store rationalised marketing in the same way that machines
had rationalised manufacture, and offered the same benefits :
lower prices for higher sales.

The Town, Geoffrey Martin, 1961

But the trend of today is that more and more shops move from
the particular to the general—the grocer selling meat and the
butcher groceries—and that the shopper relies upon self-service
instead of personal service and in place of 'soft-sell' methods
responds to the sticker label. In JARROW, as part of the plan for
redeveloping the town, a seven acre site in the central area was
cleared of sub-standard houses and its design as a major shopping
centre on a pedestrian precinct basis was entrusted to a well-
known firm of property developers. A supermarket dominates the
site. In a Midlands city the writer's recent enquiry for the where-
abouts of the market brought a direction to the supermarket : the
old market, when found, seemed to be fading out.

DERBY, with its long-established tradition of shopping, has not
yet been swamped by the new modes. On other industrial towns

the effect of mushrooming supermarkets, variety chain stores such as Woolworth's, Marks & Spencer's, and multiple shops like May-pole Dairy, Boots, Timothy White's, has been to depersonalise the whole retail exchange between customer and supplier. When, in addition, a new shopping precinct is planned and 'left to a well-known firm of property developers' the heart of the town tends to lose its physical identity. So often a 'Northern tradition of progress' goes by the board and it begins instead to resemble any of the places in the LONDON commuter belt—unless by imagina-tive flair it takes on a glorified fairground appearance like the new Bull Ring at Birmingham. Soon it begins to look and feel the same in WIGAN or WALSALL as in WATFORD or WALTHAMSTOW. Moreover in these stores the weakness of the large-scale retailer is magnified, when the customer comes into first contact with the lowest-paid workers in the establishment—a manifest disadvant-age in any trade where the customer is always right.

For years now the Co-operative movement, begun in a spirit of highminded endeavour by the Rochdale Pioneers in 1844, has been ailing, bogged down in a musty, mahoganied Victorian image.

Year by year, the CWS's profits have been sliding steadily downwards : from just over £10 million in 1956 to just under £5 million in 1965. To rub in just how badly things have been going wrong, the CWS's sales have been rising. Over the same period they are up from £444 million to £487 million.

The retail Co-operative Societies—who own and manage the CWS as well as being its customers—have been making equally heavy weather of it. 'Societies have been merging at the rate of thirty or so a year for the past four or five years' says a Co-op official, 'and you can assume that most of them are merging because they are finding the going tough'.

In the High Streets few doubt that the traditional Co-ops are taking a hiding from the supermarkets. The Co-op's retail sales, at £1,105 million, were only one per cent up in 1966 on 1965. This kind of growth is not likely to keep anyone happy —except perhaps the supermarkets.

The Observer, January 1967

As symptoms of a town's wellbeing, economically, one must not deprecate the new shopping precincts and supermarkets. Since real income rose in the later 1930s there has been wider spending than ever before, with more emphasis on clothes and household goods and on pleasures other than beer; a rise in the standard of living that has been catered for by new media of supply. But as evidence of another kind of 'conurbation'—town-fusing by commercial planning of an indistinguishable unit type—one may regard the change as a sort of convalescence from which perhaps a less cramped, more durable town will emerge ready to rebuild its character. One of the dangers is that these depersonalised architectural schemes are not only out of line but out of scale with the old town on which they are foisted. It is all too easy in the Northern town which has settled down into a comfortable, compact community of 70-80,000 people—BARNSLEY, BARROW, BURNLEY, DARLINGTON, DONCASTER, ROCHDALE, STOCKTON, WARRINGTON, WIGAN—to swamp individuality while imposing 'improvements'.

Few towns, of course, can cater for the needs of an expanding, car-shopping population in terms of nineteenth-century family retail shops. Few mining villages can afford to persist with the wooden shanty barbers' and cobblers' shops, or the fish-and-chip shops 'no more than painted sheds fitted out with frying equipment, with bottles of fizzy lemonade, limejuice and soda, dandelion and burdock standing across the bottom of the small four-paned window' (Stan Barstow). Nor will villagers put up with 'pork pies and peas served with hot sweet tea on bare wooden tables', in a covered market when they have been exposed to espresso bars and Chinese restaurants. In few towns, except some of those in the tightly-built narrow valleys of the Pennine industrial area, will it be possible for long to do what STOKE-ON-TRENT'S official handbook can do for BURSLEM, printing a street plan of the town centre with the street names of Arnold Bennett's 'Bursley', its shops and other features almost the same as in the 'Five Towns' novels' setting of Edwardian times. Even here changes are reducing the original impact of the scene: Clayhanger's Steam Printing Works is now an Indian restaurant, Critchlow's shop forms part of Woolworth's premises, a fruiterer's has replaced another printing works; but St Luke's covered market and the furniture shop of John Baines in St Luke's Square remain.

For those who value shopping tradition, the town markets and the great departmental stores offer most sense of permanence in the changing Northern cities and towns. It is to the great stores— Brown Muff's of BRADFORD (established 1814, by a packman according to tradition), Schofields of LEEDS, Ranby's of DERBY, Kendall's of MANCHESTER—that the northerner turns for prestige shopping or if he ever feels called upon to show that 'fashionwise the North is as smart as London'. 'Departments expand and contract according to season where this is helpful to the customer' announces one of these stores: 'for instance although skis are in stock all the year round, the ski-shop only blossoms into full importance in the late autumn to cater for this particular interest. In the spring this space is devoted to summer fashions. The store has excellent fashion departments, an exceptionally good man's shop and a linen department the envy of many larger organisations, yet it retains a spirit of courtesy and helpfulness, the traditions of first-class personal service, not often found these days. One is aware of the friendly atmosphere within minutes of entering'. Friendliness there is as cherished an asset as in the corner shop or market stall: astuteness with the 'brass' is up to the customer.

SCHOOL

*At certain schools he [HMI] could tell pretty accurately by the
pupils' faces how long they had been at school. The longer the
period the more stupid, vacant and expressionless the face.*

Lectures on the Science and Art of Education, Joseph Payne, 1883

*The labouring classes of a highly industrialised society, in which
every man works at a narrowly specialised task all day long,
tend to lose their mental flexibility and powers of discrimina-
tion, and thus to become easy marks for the demagogue.*

The Wealth of Nations, Adam Smith

Almost as many reasons have been offered for *not* educating as
for educating the working classes in industrial England. Which-
ever course happened to gain favour it was not a common, universal education 'planned with the simple grand purpose of
educating the people' that was envisaged. When giving education at all seemed to accord with national policy as often as not
the churches found against it, in that it was likely either to promote or to undermine the hold of one sect or another. In any
case, for the labouring class 'it is enough if every one is wise in
the working of his own craft : so best will they maintain the state
of the world' (Coleridge). For the poor, then, school was a doubtful starter.

About the turn of the eighteenth century and in the Napoleonic
era reasons were advanced for supplying some degree of elementary education at least. Among them was the belief that such
dangers as Jacobinism, machine-smashing riots, atheism, drunkenness and social unrest could be averted if, instead of being at the
mercy of demagogues who had devoured Tom Paine's *The Rights
of Man*, the millions of workers were to receive enough controlled
schooling to allow them to perceive and accept the truths of

religion and the decencies of ordered society. The workman who was able to read and number was bound to be a more productive workman, better at handling machinery, avoiding waste, perhaps even capable of devising small improvements. The fact that Methodists showed an interest in helping their members to read and write in Sunday or charity school alarmed the Anglicans into similar activity. Of course one had to be careful how one instructed the poor, in case, like the evangelical Hannah More, one were to be accused of corrupting the principles of the community. 'My object', said that lady, 'is not to make fanatics, but to train up the lower classes in habits of industry and piety.'

The machinery to further this object of limited education for the masses was run on the same lines as that in the manufactories, namely the division of labour applied to intellectual purposes. Penny-a-week schools for the poor were supported by Nonconformists and Anglicans alike. In them, mechanical instruction based very largely on the Bible—reading, writing, the first four rules of arithmetic, some history and ancient geography—could be given to hundreds of children sitting close-packed in one room under one master. Dissenters' schools came under the auspices of the British & Foreign School Society (formerly the Lancastrian Society, so called after its Quaker founder, 1808, Joseph Lancaster); Anglicans' schools came under the National Society for Promoting the Education of the Poor in the Principles of the Established Church (founder Dr Andrew Bell). Both systems were similar and like the factories, relied upon child labour. Bell actually called his schools 'the steam engines of the moral world'.[1]

At the Royal Lancastrian School, established in MANCHESTER in 1810, the curious visitor might have seen how the systems worked. Over 1,000 children sat on serried rows of benches with two masters and one mistress in charge. Each nine or ten children were placed under another child called a monitor. For a dictation lesson, the monitors, brighter children who had lately learnt the lesson themselves, at a signal from the master on the platform at one end, led off to their group with a three or four-

[1] Schools in the original National School premises may still be found, as at Bingley, Yorkshire WR.

syllabled word. And so in order, from monitor to monitor, throughout the whole assembly. When six words had been dictated and the monitor had inspected his charges' slates, he signalled back to the master by means of a 'telegraph' or sign-board fixed at the end of the bench. Corrections were made, the master signalled again and another six words were dictated. Monitors taught their group to read in a similar fashion from a board with the lesson printed upon it; they hung a sign about the neck of any pupil talking, idling or untidy, a device adapted by Dickens for the treatment of David Copperfield at Salem House.

It was the age of mechanical invention and cheap labour. Sup-posing 2,000,000 children were to be educated,' said Dr Bell; on the old plan, with schools of fifty pupils and a master's stipend of £50, the cost would work out at £1 per pupil; by his plan, with schools of 500 pupils and £50 to each master, the cost would be only 2s per pupil, a saving overall of £1,800,000. Such schools were dependent on public subscription. In private enterprise and benevolence based on the desire of each party, Church and Dissent, to control the education of the poor and so determine whether or not particular religious doctrines should be taught, one must not lose sight of economy. Cheapness meant 'multiplica-tion of utility'. In fact, schools were to go short of funds for almost another two generations, largely because of the bickering between the religious factions and their opposition to accepting Govern-mental funds with Governmental control. It was clearly impos-sible to supply the flood of schools required without public money, but before public money could be used a formula had to be found to satisfy all parties. Meanwhile the education of the workers in the new industrial cities was left to some nondescript agents, if indeed they obtained an education at all.

The degree of State interest in schooling may be measured by the first allocation of public funds for education, a grant of £20,000 towards school building, to be divided between the two above-mentioned societies. It was made in 1833 when the Factory Act which limited children's hours of work also obliged, in theory, those under thirteen to attend school for two hours a day. Where the Act's requirements did not become a dead letter, since it was virtually a tax on industry, and school facilities in factories were set up, the results could hardly be classed as 'education'. The 'schoolroom' might be a coal-hole, the teacher a fireman and the two hours regarded as a chance for the 'pupils' to sit down and rest. Out of 500 mills in the West Riding, 300-400 used this 'short-time' labour, but an official reporting in 1839 'could not name a dozen schools where the education is systematically good and the mill-owner personally cognisant of the progress of his children'.

⚬⚬⚬

Of DAME SCHOOLS—ramshackle, self-supporting schools for those who could afford to pay 3d or 4d a week—there were 230 in MANCHESTER in the period 1834-7.

'The old fashioned type where a tidy old lady would teach habits of neatness, even though her literary standards were not high'; or 'kept by a blind man who hears his scholars their lessons and explains them with great simplicity'; or, quite as probably, 'a dirty, close room where children were sent not so much to learn as to be taken care of and out of the way at home; where books to read and fresh air to breathe were equally scarce, where discipline depended on the rod, where the only saving grace was a certain slackness so that in hot weather, for instance, the children could stretch out their limbs (provided there were room) on forms or floor, and sleep away the weary afternoon. . . . Teaching might be combined with keeping a cake shop, for which the pupils provided a clientèle, or with selling milk'.

COMMON DAY SCHOOLS charging 6d or 9d a week, and run by teachers whose qualification for the job was apparently their unfitness for every other, supplied the next stage for learning the elements of the three R's together with penmanship and perhaps some grammar and geography for 'extras'.

The Bleak Age, J. L. and Barbara Hammond, 1947

The Dame School tradition goes back at least a century before this: Fanny Hill's mother kept 'a little day-school for the girls in her neighbourhood' at a small village near Liverpool, where Fanny's education, 'no better than very vulgar', consisted of reading 'or rather spelling an illegible scrawl' and 'a little ordinary plainwork' till she was past fourteen.

Memoirs of Fanny Hill, John Cleland, 1749

⚬⚬⚬

In LEEDS there were 154 day schools, including Dame Schools, and 20 factory schools. Altogether about 6,750 children attended them: another 11,400 attended the 50 Sunday Schools. But 4,500 working-class children under the age of nine had no instruction in day schools at all. And, in the second report of the Children's Employment Commission (1843), it was calculated that of the 11,000 children covered by the inspection at least seventy-five per cent would leave school 'unable to read the Scriptures with tolerable ease or correctness'. In the swollen factory cities of the North, until well after mid-century, hundreds of thousands of children never attended school at all. In MANCHESTER in 1833 more than a third of all the children aged between five and fifteen were found not to be at school; in LIVERPOOL more than half. In the working-class districts of MANCHESTER in 1867 some thirty-five per cent of the children were found never to have attended school; in LIVERPOOL in 1871 the proportion was one-quarter of those of school age. The situation in LEEDS and BIR-MINGHAM was little better.

The influence ranged against educating the poor, even to the extent of removing the hindrance of illiteracy in factory hands or trying to reduce the incidence of juvenile delinquency, as the Sunday Schools tried to do, was insidious. Putting ideas into working-class heads would be sure to breed discontent, if not actual revolt. Teaching the children to read was playing with fire, since propaganda for atheism and sedition was as easy to read as the Scriptures. Reading 'romances' on the other hand might lead to a taste for luxury and idleness and to the workhouse, instead of the workshop. The agricultural interests expressed anxiety about their continuing supply of cheap field labour : 'the ranks of society upon which the general happiness of the lower orders no less than of those that are more elevated depends' feared upheaval. When the State attempted to improve education (1843), in the first instance for factory children but with the hope that it would apply to all children in the factory districts, the hostility of Nonconformists to any scheme which might injure their Sunday Schools and give the Established Church too much say, caused the scheme to be dropped. Illiteracy remained at forty to forty-one per cent as measured by the Registrar General's records among marrying persons (1846). Repeal of the Corn Laws seemed light amusement, said Cobden, 'compared with the difficult task of inducing priests of all denominations to suffer the people to be educated'.

By 1861 the Government felt prepared to improve existing schools, but not to grasp English education firmly and remould it into a national scheme. The sum of £26,000,000 was budgeted for the Army and Navy; £813,441 sufficed for education. Even so, clamour for economy, for not wasting money on ineffective education, led to a 'payment by results' scheme for all elementary schools receiving subsidy. Before obtaining any further grant each school had to show by examination results that it had used its annual amount to maximum advantage. So children were condemned to another treadmill, taking prescribed subjects in a given year, learning by rote from fixed lesson books and reproducing the sentences and facts required by the inspector at year end—on pain of losing 2s 8d per subject to the school for each pupil's failure! The scheme appeared to work: Government aid to schools was reduced to £636,000. Of what concern was it if the nation's poorer children hated their schooldays and, while almost ninety per cent passed the reading tests after drill upon a single book for a year, gave up all reading as soon as they left school? Robert Lowe, vice-president of the Education Committee and deviser of the scheme, had the answer: 'The lower classes ought to be educated to discharge the duties cast upon them. We do not profess to give these children an education which will raise them above their station and business in life—that is not our object.'

The Reform Bill of 1867, which doubled the electorate and left the workers holding the balance of political power, re-emphasised the need of schools for the masses. 'We must educate our masters' became the new slogan, but quantity, not quality of literacy was the main aim. All along the masses continued to be regarded as so many units of society, not as individual persons with their own intellectual and emotional needs. Three years after the Reform Bill the Forster Act at last paved the way for a national system of schools; the Government was to take responsibility for education where voluntary effort was not adequate. School, therefore, became less easy to avoid and slum children were subject, like others, to being taught to read. But for long the demands of examination and rote memory work killed any joy to be had in it.

ϾᏔᎣ

The Education Act of 1870 was not an Act for a common universal education, it was an Act to educate the lower classes for employment on lower-class lines and with specially trained, inferior teachers who had no university quality. . . .

The National Schools in spirit, form and intention were inferior schools and to send one's children to them was a definite and final acceptance of social inferiority.

An Experiment in Autobiography, H. G. Wells, 1934

ϾᏔᎣ

The great Northern cities were ready to act on the decision that local authorities should supplement voluntary effort for schooling. MANCHESTER was operating a scheme to provide free breakfasts of bread, milk and coffee to poor children in their fifteen 'Board' schools by 1876,[1] on the principle that hungry children make poor scholars. But it was the constant complaint of HMIs that, apart from the Bible, children had no *humanising* instruction at all. 'The whole use that the Government makes of the mighty engine of literature in the education of the working classes amounts to little more, even when most successful, than giving them the power to read the newspapers.' (Matthew Arnold: *Report on Elementary Schools*.) The ideas of utilitarianism clung like ivy—echoes of Gradgrind's words to M'Choakumchild: 'Teach these boys and girls nothing but facts. Facts alone are wanted in life. Plant nothing else and root out everything else' rang through the second half of the century.

ϾᏔᎣ

Teachers also suffered from lack of humanising training methods and from the premium set upon rote memory and graduated examinations. Under the Government Normal Schools (dating from 1840), 'Mr M'Choakumchild and some one hundred and forty other schoolmasters, had been lately turned at the same time, in the same factory, on the same

[1] In 1960 the same authority supplied over 50,000 daily school meals.

principles, like so many pianoforte legs. He had been put through an immense variety of paces, and had answered volumes of head-breaking questions. Orthography, etymology, syntax, and prosody, biography, astronomy, geography, and general cosmography, the sciences of compound proportion, algebra, land-surveying and levelling, vocal music and drawing from models, were all at the end of his ten chilled fingers. He had worked his stony way into Her Majesty's most Honourable Privy Council's Schedule B, and had taken the bloom off the higher branches of mathematics and physical science, French, German, Latin and Greek. He knew all about the watersheds of the world (whatever they are), and all the histories of all the peoples, and all the names of all the rivers and mountains, and all the productions, manners, and customs of all the countries, and all their boundaries and bearings on the two and thirty points of the compass. Ah, rather overdone, M'Choakumchild. If he had only learned a little less—how infinitely better he might have taught much more.'

Hard Times, Charles Dickens, 1854

Scientific facts as food for the rising generation and key to success in life formed the core of the age's educational theory. The elementary school with classes numbering up to seventy and with half-time workers free to leave at the age of ten (some measure of half-time attendance still went on in the 20s) had little time or chance for anything more than rudimentary handing out of facts, morning hymn, scripture lesson, reading, writing and arithmetic, needlework for girls, 'bills of parcels' for advanced pupils, copying of copper-plate maxims, these were the staple subjects. When the nation awoke to the commercial threat from America and the continent, in particular to Germany's rapid advance and superior standards of education, it was in scientific instruction that hopes of recovery were placed. The idea of the secondary technical schooling blossomed from a mere six laboratories in 1873 to organised Science Schools with more than a thousand within the next thirty years.

In this characteristic Victorian innovation the impact of Darwin and Huxley was felt, but it took more than that to leaven the Latin and Greek curriculum of the old endowed grammar

schools with new ideas. (LEEDS Grammar School had tried, in
vain, to introduce modern subjects, such as English, in 1805 :
until after 1840 such schools were forbidden to modernise and
were obliged to remain faithful to their foundation instruments,
often Tudor in origin.) Classics for the middle and professional
classes—as in the public schools for the sons of successful manufacturers—long remained the thing : their residual appeal is felt
in those quarters still, if only as snob-culture.

❧

A voice in the wilderness :
I believe that a girl's education, should be nearly, in its
course and material of study, the same as a boy's; but quite
differently directed. A woman, in any rank of life, ought to
know whatever her husband is likely to know, but to know
it in a different way. His command of it should be foundational
and progressive; hers, general and accomplished for daily and
helpful use. Not but that it would often be wiser in men to
learn things in a womanly sort of way, for present use, and to
seek for the discipline and training of their mental powers in
such branches of study, as will afterwards be fittest for social
service; but, speaking broadly, a man ought to know any
language or science he learns, thoroughly—while a woman
ought to know the same language, or science, only so far as
may enable her to sympathise in her husband's pleasure, and
in those of his best friends. . . .
Not only in the material and in the course, but yet more
earnestly in the spirit of it, let a girl's education be as serious
as a boy's. You bring up your girls as if they were meant for
sideboard ornaments and then complain of their frivolity . . .
there is hardly a girls' school in this Christian kingdom where
the children's courage or sincerity would be thought of half
so much importance as their way of coming in at a door. . . .
And give them, lastly, not only noble teachings, but noble
teachers. Is a girl likely to think her own conduct, or her own
intellect, of much importance, when you trust the entire formation of her character, moral and intellectual, to a person
whom you let your servants treat with less respect than they
do your housekeeper?   Sesame and Lilies, John Ruskin, 1865

❧

It accorded with nineteenth-century principles that schools should be graded according to the social class they served. There was an escape route—or 'fire escape' it has been called—for exceptionally able children of the poorest classes from the lower to the higher institutions. The School Board provided a number of scholarships for elementary children to these schools for the well-to-do, but it was little more than a token escape. In MANCHESTER before 1900 a total of a hundred of these free places were offered to elementary children each year, a ratio of about one to ten in the competition of suitable candidates. Of the 30,000 pupils then in grammar schools altogether barely one per cent came by scholarships from elementary schools. This theory of the educational ladder as a means to a wider democracy was suspect in some circles as being little more than the seduction of the ablest members of the working class into the ruling class. On a domestic and social level its risks in terms of class loyalties and contentment were often as great as its wider opportunities.

Any case of 'Unwillingly to school' could not fairly be blamed upon working-class children or their parents until Victorian emphasis on the four Rs (including Religion) gave place to encouragement in elementary schools of more natural activities of hand and eye. With many adults, however, it was a case of 'willingly' as soon as facilities for schooling were obtained. The common belief at the outset of the nineteenth century that the 'education of the ordinary people was economically unsound and socially destructive' did not ultimately prevent the setting up of Mechanics' Institutes in most northern towns—although Anglican clergy were long hostile. Such critics were sure that if science and political economy were taught to mechanics and labourers, the institutes would become 'Jacobin clubs and nurseries of disaffection' or else breeding houses of freethinkers and atheists.

After the foundation of the London Mechanics' Institute, 1823, and with the support of one of its founders, Lord Brougham, the larger industrial communities went rapidly ahead with theirs— LEEDS in 1824, KEIGHLEY, BRADFORD, WAKEFIELD, DEWSBURY, HALIFAX, HUDDERSFIELD by the end of 1825. By mid-century nearly all the towns of south-east Lancashire had their institutes,

with classes and lectures, libraries and newsrooms; and over a
score of places in Yorkshire had erected their own buildings. One
can visualise their heyday—solid, stone-faced Victorian-Gothic
buildings—if one looks twice at many a municipal library or
former technical school in a textile town, and one can realise their
apogee in MANCHESTER's Mechanics' Institute, ancestor of the
present College of Science & Technology. The rules of Mechanics'
Institutes originally banned both political and religious discussion,
books and newspapers, in order to placate those who viewed with
feigned alarm the 'assembling periodically of several hundred of
the labouring classes'. Emphasis was placed on popularising
scientific knowledge; but as many artisans could neither read nor
write, the institutes had to act as glorified elementary schools as
well. 'The patient leaders taught them with facts; after the first
flush of excitement, however, the dry details of scientific lore, of
hydrostatics and pneumatics and aerostatics, proved either beyond the grasp or insufficient to arouse the continued enthusiasm
of jaded artisans. Then alarm of a different sort arose, about the
prospects of institutes. Apart from the élite of their class, working
men tended to shy away from the larger institutes with their air
of patronage, preferring instead their own small self-help societies
—such as the Leeds Mutual Improvement Society (begun 1844).
(In the prologue to 'The Princess' Tennyson describes in detail
a borough institute outing to the grounds of its titled patron.)

Rules and Regulations, Leeds Mechanics' Institute (1824) :
The object of the Mechanics' Institute is to supply, at a
cheap rate, to the different classes of the community, the
advantages of instruction in the various branches of science,
which are of practical application to their several trades or
occupations. Such instruction cannot fail to prove of important
use to every workman, who is employed in any mechanical, or
chemical, operation; and the scientific instruction, which will
give a more thorough knowledge of their arts, will greatly tend
to improve the skill and practice of those classes of men, who
are so essentially conducive to the prosperity of this large
manufacturing town.
This object is to be obtained by the circulation of a well-

L

selected collection of books, in the various branches of science, which are applicable to the useful arts—by instruction in the higher branches of Arithmetic, Mathematics, Mechanical Drawing, and the Principles of Mechanics and Chemistry, to be given in the evenings by competent masters, to such members or scholars as are desirous of forming classes for that purpose—by models of machines to be kept in a room of the Society appropriated to that purpose, and by premiums offered by the Society—by Chemical Apparatus, and Instruments applicable to the advancement of the Arts, to be gradually collected as the funds of the Society will permit—by Public Lectures on Mechanics and Chemistry, and other branches of science, which are immediately applicable to, or connected with, the useful Arts, and more especially in their application to the different processes of the manufactures of this town.

So the MI classes and lectures were attended mainly by clerks, foremen, businessmen instead of the packers, carters, millhands for whom they had been intended. And instead of courses of scientific knowledge Penny Readings and popular lectures on history, travel, biography, music, literature were gradually introduced—thinly disguised amusement for the middle classes. The career of Dickens, as a dramatic lecturer, began at the Birmingham Midland Institute in 1853. Working men felt increasingly out of place on this cultural fringe; *they* would have preferred political discussion about their 'rights' over a pipe and a pot of beer to talks on the principles of the steam engine. 'After working at wheels all day they ought not to be made to study wheels at night' too. In Yorkshire the MI movement retained a membership of over 60,000 until well into the 90s. The institute libraries, supplied later, were an inducement to some, the newsrooms to others. But in general the exodus of the mechanics left the institutes as social centres, with chess and billiards and theatricals, and, sometimes, a neglected corner where careful brass models of pumps and steam engines and steam hammers gathered dust long after they had ceased to attract even boys. Occasionally the institute became the nucleus of a 'polytechnic'.

Various other schemes for adult schooling enjoyed more success.

In SHEFFIELD Charist ideals led to a People's College, 1842, which provided workmen with language and literature courses at 9d per student. Rochdale Pioneers' Co-operative began educational work that emerged eventually in the Manchester College. At ANCOATS, MANCHESTER and SALFORD working men's colleges produced a merger with Owen's College (founded 1851), which preserved the future MANCHESTER university. Then the idea of university extension courses, begun in Cambridge in 1873, was taken up by the Victoria University, Manchester, in the following decade, with weekly or fortnightly lectures and classes for the more serious students in subjects taught in the university itself. In addition MANCHESTER evolved a system of Evening Continuation Schools—the now ubiquitous 'night school'. Many extension courses, like MI lectures, tended to be taken over by middle-class supporters; but in NORTHUMBERLAND one course, on political economy, attracted 1,300 miners and kept its hold in later series with other subjects also.

Best known and best patronised, perhaps, of the adult schools was the WEA. Workers Education was regarded by its keenest supporters as education for political and economic power, both local and national, in order to achieve work and leisure and security. Backed by socially-minded Oxford dons and inspired by a Co-operative Wholesale Society clerk from Whitechapel, Albert Mansbridge, the WEA movement of 1903 soon took root in the North. Three of the first ten branches were formed in Lancashire, at ROCHDALE (1904), DARWEN, and BOLTON. Yorkshire branches at WAKEFIELD and SHEFFIELD followed in 1906; the year after at LEEDS, YORK, DEWSBURY, TODMORDEN: then at HUDDERSFIELD, BRADFORD, HALIFAX.

Well before the First World War, tutorial classes had an enthusiastic following. From eighteen to thirty-two men and women met for two hours a week during three winter seasons, to study a non-vocational subject, usually in economics, local government, or economic history, under a qualified, university-appointed tutor. Class and teacher were often deeply united in their desire for an educated democracy: they shared a social purpose and pooled their knowledge and experience: the class was itself a self-governing unit. In addition, holiday schools, such as those held at Whitsuntide at Ingleton high among the Pennines and in summer at Saltburn on the north Yorkshire coast, helped to foster district patriotism and sense of fellowship. The writer was privileged to be present when Arthur Greenwood, MP, an early inspirer of the Yorkshire WEA, received a send-off from his visit to the school at Ingleton with the whole company singing 'For He's a Jolly Good Fellow' on the bridge over the river at midnight.

The quality of class entrants to the WEA was high at first—creamed from the mutual improvement societies, Sunday Schools and cottage reading groups. Later, although branch activities were still devoted to 'education for social and industrial emancipation', as the idea of the WEA spread it lost something of its early spirit and quality. Subjects other than the social sciences crept in to the tutorial courses: shorter and less exacting courses in literature, music, local history, French, folk dancing, psychology, were demanded by and supplied to people who, after 1924, did not require to enrol as branch members in order to join a class. In fact popular culture largely took over from social purpose. Since 1944 the WEA has found itself in the main, like the LEAs which help to support it, a universal provider.

School, until the end of the nineteenth century, virtually ceased for the masses at the elementary stage, with a bonus perhaps of what could be picked up in night school after experience in the 'University of Hard Knocks'. The State opened the door to secondary education for all in 1902, when a scholarship entry of at least twenty-five per cent to grammar and secondary schools receiving public aid was laid down. In MANCHESTER, for instance, instead of the hundred free places offered to elementary children before the opening of the century, there were by 1924 1,400 free places; but there were still six suitable candidates for every place. Until that date no completely new secondary school was built by that city, although some central schools were renamed 'high schools'. Up to 1944, when an Education Act came into force much more generous than previous Acts in advancing the principle of equality of educational opportunity in the State system (and also making it the duty of each LEA to provide for further education for those over school age willing to profit by it), schools were still graded broadly according to the social class and career probability of their pupils. The secondary schools were for the professions, central and junior technical schools for artisans and lower-middle-class jobs, senior schools for the unskilled and labouring class after the age of eleven.

Yet with all its competitive strain the ladder of educational opportunity was notably easier of access than at the end of the previous century. Well before the Second World War three-quarters of secondary-school pupils came from the elementary schools; and in the universities, taking in 'Oxbridge' as well as 'Redbrick', about forty per cent of the students had mounted the same ladder, coming from the smaller grammar schools as well as from those with scholastic reputations like Bradford, Manchester, Newcastle. In at least one of the latter half-hearted attempts were made to ensure that the Northern boy of humbler origin was not at a disadvantage when he reached the privileged society of 'Oxbridge', by sixth-form masters giving a few tips on dining etiquette, dress and how not to pronounce 'bath' and 'mother' : but in general it was assumed, rightly or wrongly, that ability and application would see one through.

❦

Provincial universities :

Bill goes off five mornings a week to Redbrick University exactly as he went to Back Street Council School and Drab-town Municipal Secondary School for Boys—and he goes on his bicycle to save the twopenny tram fare. Exactly as at those earlier institutions, he climbs the similar flights of dirty, sordid stairs (only there are more of them), sits in a rather larger class-room of the same type and with the same grimy outlook and answers to his name called from very much the same kind of register. His lunch consists, according to the state of his finances, of a shilling made-up meat-dish, or of a roll and a cup of coffee, taken hurriedly at the University Union and followed by the meeting of some society sandwiched between lunch and after-noon lectures because no society that meets in the late after-noon can hope for more than the most diminutive attendance. Between four and five o'clock he goes home to the same sort of high tea as he has had all his life and then attempts to settle down to an evening's work, in an unused sitting-room, his unheated bedroom or, more probably, in the living-room. . . .

Each block of the university buildings (erected during the late Victorian or early Edwardian epochs in LEEDS, BIRMINGHAM, LIVERPOOL, SHEFFIELD) of light stone which the coal-dust of the city quickly turned to a dismal and depressing grey or of a hideously cheerful red brick, was like a glorified technical school, with a common room perhaps for the staff, but certainly none for the undergraduates. If they wanted to dance they had to clear some lecture room of tables or desks and foot it featly under the auspices of statues of the ancient gods or in an atmosphere perfumed with Sulphuretted hydrogen.

Redbrick University, Bruce Truscot, 1943

Standards of architecture, accommodation, amenities, staffing and tuition have in most cases greatly improved since this account.

❧

The corresponding drawbacks to this were felt in the elementary schools, which had to grind away at English and arithmetic and concentrate on the cream of their pupils to the detriment of the rest, while fighting for secondary places: and in the crowded timetables, the Latin and language burden, the Matriculation straightjacket of secondary schools priding themselves on the university places they could achieve. Practical activities and local interests, wide reading and individual studies, nature walks and schools visits all felt the 'squeeze' in the struggle to produce intellectual all-rounders. 'Children must be placed not according to their fathers' conditions but the faculties of their minds.' The dictum is Plato's; the direction of educational thought since the Second World War stems from it. Equality of opportunity within the State system now has its blueprint in comprehensive schools. No longer the separatism, even on occupational lines of grammar, technical and secondary modern school: no longer, if planners succeed, the private public-school system for the (financially) élite. Social inequalities, such as those found to obtain in MIDDLESBROUGH grammar schools (in 1953), where analysis showed that one in three of the sons of clerical workers obtained a place compared with only one in eight of working-class boys, when the full quota of places for those succeeding in the tests were available—such inequalities must no longer be seen to be perpetuated by the State.[1] That all under one roof should be treated on equal terms according to their faculties is the new order.

The dream, with its nightmare corollary, destruction of the grammar schools—although it reflects a wide-spread consciousness of the value of schooling without class limitations and the uneasy privileges of the past—may have a rude awakening; but at any rate the roofs can be mended properly. Northern authorities are well aware that children in school have all too long lived in too large classes, in premises too old and out of date, in surroundings too congested, noisy, and dirty. After the end of the Second World War the building of new schools, especially secondary modern and technical, to fit in with the interim policy of planning secondary education according to pupils' aims, aptitudes and abilities, had priority in many areas. Fine-looking schools resulted, with expensive, almost luxurious extras before economy cuts in building were reimposed. Towns in some formerly depressed areas were able to pride themselves on their educational facilities. 'The standard and educational range in the town (of WORKINGTON) and the county's generous scheme of awards to students are such that every child can receive the education best suited to his needs and have every opportunity of proceeding to college or University' *(Official Guide)*. 'The Grammar School occupies a spacious functional building opened in 1954 and equipped with excellent hall, gymnasium, science laboratories, workshops and canteen. . . . The WORKINGTON College of Further Education is extending rapidly and a new block of lecture rooms and laboratories was recently completed; the College is particularly strong in electrical, mining and chemical engineering, as well as various trade, mechanical and cultural studies.'

As in the North-West so also in the North-East. GATESHEAD

[1] The Minister of State for Education & Science was able to say, in November 1967, that more than twenty-six per cent of our university population was now drawn from the working class.

local education authority has been in the process of 'implement-
ing an extensive school development plan since the war and when
the new building for the Boys' Grammar School is opened in the
near future, this plan will be completed in respect of grammar
and secondary technical education, as by then all four schools
will have been housed in modern, well-equipped and spacious
buildings' *(Guide)*.

Comprehensivisation, ugly term, using present buildings in new
ways or causing new, and ever more factory-like, schools to be
built, may break down some of the class anomalies between
grammar and other types of secondary school; but it leads to much
heart-burning and dilution of hardly-won standards of achieve-
ment, as well as to rejoicing in level-at-any-price circles. Hasty
change is wasteful change: a quantitative measure seems again
to be ousting qualitative standards of school education. In one
respect, however, both haste and change appear relative terms.
LANCASHIRE has currently 430 primary schools built over a hundred years ago. Most of them are in the old industrial areas: all
need replacing. At the present rate of replacement—four or five
per year—it will take another seventy-five years to deal with this
problem alone. As to overcrowding, there are in such schools
nearly 1,300 classes with from forty to fifty children in each, and
twenty-two classes with over fifty children. In all the primary
classes about one-fifth remain oversized.

To get the 'feel' of such premises and their environments the
writer suggests a look at WIGAN, where pockets of old planning
remain alongside many fine new developments. In the congeries
of mean streets between Miry Lane and Chapel Lane south of
the railway stations and north of the canal—all blackened brick
and cindery waste ground, back-to-back houses with living rooms
draped in drying clothes, dim, struggling, half-stocked little shops
from which grey, shrunken women in clogs emerge carrying quart
jugs and try to breast the stream of lorries—there stand a Church
of England and a Roman Catholic infant school, St Thomas's
and St Joseph's. The latter at least is scheduled for replacement:
the play-yard view through spiked railings of a colossal factory
chimney could be straight out of an industrial scene by Doré. Just

round the corner children scramble about a pool of cindery water and a pile of broken bricks. Wigan—a spa in the eighteenth century—is not the only place with these warts to cure.

'Education is concerned primarily with the welfare of each individual, recognising at the same time its responsibility to the industrial and commercial life of the city.' The definition of education coined by MANCHESTER Education Committee (1938) asks for 'primarily' to be inscribed in letters of red wherever the blueprints of a new super-structure are being turned into bricks and mortar. Parts of the North still face the problems of a hundred years ago, crowded schools, cramped children, near-slum conditions: but now the State is awake to these problems. At the time of writing the Plowden Report on primary education has newly exposed the old inadequacies and also given precise prescriptions for what needs to be done.

How far is it possible to improve the quality of education within schools without also raising the quality of living in the homes from which the children come? Not only is increase in public spending on the improvement of the schools in slum areas required; if children come from a bad neighbourhood and a poor home background they will have correspondingly less chance of doing well at school, in spite of a recommended national system of nursery schools. So the logical conclusion is for 'educational priority areas' to be treated as 'social priority areas' and for improvements in education to march alongside improvements in housing and all other facilities. Otherwise it seems 'the forces operating outside the school walls (which) are more persuasive and more powerful than those within it' will continue to be so.

෴

From AN ELEMENTARY SCHOOL CLASSROOM IN A SLUM :

On sour cream walls, donations. Shakespeare's head
Cloudless at dawn, civilized dome riding all cities.
Belled, flowery, Tyrolese valley. Open-handed map
Awarding the world its world. And yet, for these
Children, these windows, not this world, are world,
Where all their future's painted with a fog,

A narrow street sealed in a lead sky,
Far far from rivers, capes and stars of words.

Surely Shakespeare is wicked, the map a bad example
With ships and sun and love tempting them to steal—
For lives that slyly turn in their cramped holes
From fog to endless night? On their slag heap, these children
Wear skins peeped through by bones and spectacles of steel
With mended glass, like bottle bits on stones.
All of their time and spice are foggy slum
So blot their maps with sums as big as doom.

Stephen Spender, 1939

CHAPEL

---

*If members of a religious persuasion built a chapel in Coke-
town—as members of eighteen religious persuasions had done—
they made it a pious warehouse of red brick. You saw nothing
in Coketown but what was severely workful.*

Hard Times, Charles Dickens, 1854

*Methodism has meant an unnecessary century and a half of
social and economic slavery for our people.*

Introducing the Arnisons, a study of middle-class Nonconformist life,
Edward Thompson, 1935

*As schools of practical democracy and self government the
Methodist chapels rendered inestimable service to the working class movement.*

Learning and Living, Prof J. F. C. Harrison, 1961

The working classes of the North of England were—and to some
extent are—essentially chapel folk. Of the various forms of dissent
they show an early and marked preference for Wesleyan
Methodism.

In Yorkshire, for example, by the end of the eighteenth century
Methodism was firmly established and by the middle of the nineteenth was regarded as the traditional religion of the West Riding.
A census taken on a Sunday in March 1851 showed a total of
983,423 church attendances for the whole county, its population
then being 1,789,047. Of these attendances over 600,000 were
at dissenting places of worship and out of that number some
431,000 attended Methodist chapels, including Primitive and
New Connection. While the number of Anglican churches in the
manufacturing districts of the West Riding was being doubled,
from 87 to 167, in the same period of less than forty-five years,

dissenting chapels had their number multiplied more than five-fold from 116 to 617.

In some strongholds such as HALIFAX the rate at which Dissent overhauled Anglicanism was even greater. Baptist, Unitarian, Independent (later called Congregational) chapels shared in this predominance, but their membership was more largely middle class. To the working class, even though in cities and big towns many artisans remained indifferent to 'the problem of spiritual culture', Nonconformity made its appeal in the form of Methodism.

Industry and Dissent : the two went together in a special way, both in the workman's and in the master-manufacturer's life. Commercial and industrial expansion during the eighteenth century came largely from the energy of Nonconformists; excluded from or liable to prejudice in public careers because of their religious opinions, they concentrated their energies and ambitions into business affairs. The founders of some of the great metal industries were men whose fathers had suffered from the intolerance of the Acts of Uniformity, which barred all non-Anglicans from holding school or university positions, or who had so suffered themselves, and sought refuge in unincorporated cities like MANCHESTER and BIRMINGHAM. Individualist religion—with its freedom from credal beliefs and ecclesiastical hierarchies, its right of private judgment—and individualist commercialism—in which getting-on replaced the enjoyments commonly accepted in public spheres—produced self-reliant men. They were also men whose attention was focused on one side of life to the exclusion of most others : preoccupation with strict morality and machine industry was not likely to encourage ideas, art or beauty, as duly testified by the factory towns of the North.

This type of evangelical religion, in contrast to the latitudinarian habit of the Established Church of the day, gained momentum from the threat offered by French Republican atheism, which threatened also established privileges and possessions. Licence and latitudinarian habits were seen as almost seditious; virtue and Sunday observance as signs of patriotism. The change survived the return of peace in 1815 and came to form the basis of Vic-

torian family life, spreading upward from merchant's household
to country-house dinner tables. Lower-class horror of atheism
especially benefited Methodism, which after Wesley's death
(1791) gained strength at the expense of the more liberal spirit
of older Nonconformist sects, whether Unitarian or Baptist. It
was this narrower, vigorously proselytising Methodism which
undertook missionary work in the industrial districts, for which
the Established Church had neither the zeal nor the organisation.
A generation elapsed before the Church of England began to
come to grips with the needs of the new towns and established
its first diocese in the West Riding.

In a period when the handloom weaver could earn perhaps
12s a week and the vicar of an industrial town such as HALIFAX
enjoyed £1,500 a year, many working men were not merely
indifferent but positively hostile to the Church of England.
Socially privileged and worldly, politically high Tory, spiritually
subservient to erastianism—a doctrine of the complete subordination of ecclesiastical to secular power—its ministers were not
equipped to bridge the gulf between rectory and artisan's cottage.
The workman could not respond to the liturgy, the ritual and
sermons delivered by a scholar and gentleman in a class-conscious
parish church. He could at least feel at home in the humble
chapel or cottage meeting-house where a local preacher, himself
a working man, expounded the same doctrine in simple, homely
fashion.

ᕯᕰᕣ

Consider the difference between the motives for building
Methodist chapels and those for building Unitarian, Independent, and even Baptist places of worship. The latter were built
for congregations versed in theology, to hear the Word of God
from ministers who held similar views on the Word to those of
the congregation.

When John Wesley died in 1791 there were 60,000 Methodists in Great Britain. These people were mostly men who had
not previously bothered about spiritual matters; they were
workers from early and dismal industrial districts, half starved
people who saw no hope of ease and happiness in this life and
were attracted by the promises of indescribable ease and

happiness in the next. When Wesley or Whitfield lifted their voices, people fell down with groans and wrestled with the Evil One.

The first chapels to be built by the Methodists were meant to serve as overflow preaching houses when the Established Church was either too far distant, too hostile, or too small in seating capacity for the numbers attracted by the new preaching. They were designed to seat as many people as possible within a good view of the pulpit. Crosses, altars and decorations were regarded as unnecessary.

First and Last Loves, John Betjeman, 1952

The cleavage was largely social. If, for instance, the working man aspired to take an active part in the organisation and control of his church it was unlikely that he could be yoked in harness with the middle-class, graduate, Anglican parson. From suspicion of their role—and of the whole discipline of a Church too exclusively adapted to the educated—beneficed clergymen were nicknamed by the lower classes the 'black dragoons' of the possessing classes. The same attitude persists even nowadays; many a labourer's wife considers the Church 'an institution for helping the "haves" against the "have-nots" '. In Nonconformist circles the position was different. Chapel gave working men a chance to study the Bible closely and to learn to speak and to organise, to persuade and to place trust in their fellows. Baptists and Wesleyans alike found occasions there for the development of talents and gratification of instincts denied expression elsewhere. The Little Bethels both fostered and themselves benefited from qualities and effort later devoted by working-class leaders to trades unions, or co-operative and political activities. The eloquence and self-control of chapel or camp meeting, the techniques of organisation and management, proved equally useful in handling mass meetings of Short Timers or of Chartists.

The role of 'plain honest workmen in their good sorts who spoke a language and a dialect we felt at home with; the fervour of the brethren who spontaneously led us in prayer; the Sunday School teachers who saw a vision of heaven in terms of real life', were usually sincerely motivated, if as clearly restricted. Methodism, allowing men to 'speak to their condition', allowed them to keep their daily thoughts and actions, social and political hopes, in the same compartments as their religion. In a sense it was a case of the poor helping the poor, except that in a chapel connection it was likely to be the poorly-educated laying down the law for the rest. The class leader, such perhaps as the LEEDS draper 'loud in his praying, rather bold in his manner, but very ignorant', helped to produce converts by the force of his fervour, but left them in a somewhat doubtful philosophical or intellectual resting place.

> I am a local preacher,
> My name is on the Plan.
> Jehovah is my teacher,
> I am a happy man.

When in due course the Plan came to contain a BA or two from Owen's College, MANCHESTER, and a visitor remarked on the Connection's good fortune, a voice from the local preachers' ranks is said to have roared out 'What's all this about your B Hays and your Hem Hays? H'im a B Hay and a Hem Hay. Hi'm Born Hagain and Marvellously Haltered.' The discipline 'whereby the souls of the Just are, sometimes to their intense vexation, made perfect on this earth in order that they may take out their letters and live and die in good standing' was, as Private Learoyd found, a strait and jealously guarded one—a fact which Kipling may have discovered from his own Methodist forebears in SKIPTON, Yorkshire.

While it can reasonably be claimed that 'close and enthusiastic study of the Bible educated the imagination' and was certainly better for the aspirant workman than so much of the reading matter that has since replaced it, the pride of early Primitive Methodists[1] in being 'one book' people is less easily defended. Exclusion of all other reading—a habit noted by Seebohm Rowntree as still to be found among chapel-going labourers even after the Second World War—or the careful restriction of reading,

---

[1] This sect originated at TUNSTALL, Staffordshire.

encouraged anti-intellectual attitudes and put a further premium on the narrow outlook. To evangelicals, reading the Bible daily was part of the programme of truly enlightened life. But performance of such reading as mere ritual, without comprehension, among the humblest classes was almost encouraged when so much other reading matter was put beyond the pale.

❧

Conflict between the Established church and Dissent is often shown in the novels of the period to hinge upon Bible reading.

'Very oft he (the Rector) comes into a house o'purpose to reprove folk for not coming to church, or not kneeling and standing when other folks does, or going to the Methody chapel, or summut o' that sort but I can't say 'at he ever fund much fault wi' me. He came to see me once or twice when I was so ill troubled in my mind. I was sore distressed, Miss Grey, but when I took my Bible, I could get no comfort of it at all. All seemed to condemn me and to show me 'at I was not in the right way; and as I knew not how to get into it, I sent to beg Mr Hatfield to be as kind as look in on me some day; and when he came I told him all my troubles'.

'And what did he say, Nancy?'

'Why, miss, he seemed like to scorn me . . . and I saw a bit of a smile on his face and he said, "Oh it's all stuff. You've been among the Methodists, my good woman". But I told him I'd never been near the Methodies. And then he said— "Well", says he, "you must come to church, where you'll hear the Scriptures properly explained, instead of sitting poring over your Bible at home".'

Agnes Grey, Anne Brontë, 1847

❧

For too long preaching the three Rs—Ruin, Redemption, Regeneration—took precedence over teaching full use and enjoyment of the other three Rs. This singleness of mind even obstructed Government proposals in 1843 to provide education for all children in factory districts; the Nonconformists raised a storm because their Sunday Schools might suffer and because they foresaw the Church having too much say in the proposals. To education in general terms the sects were not opposed: a Wesleyan

Sunday School, in Bradford, itself attacked earlier critics who argued that 'education would make the lower orders of society less disposed to submit to constituted authorities and to act in a subordinate capacity'. But as a writer of Methodist upbringing in SOUTH SHIELDS has recalled, 'Religion had a slightly dampening effect on our spirits: life was real, life was earnest indeed' (James Kirkup).

In the Aenons, Hebrons and Zions, the Elims and Salems, Bethesdas, Immanuels, and Ebenezers, the Mount Tabors, Mount Pleasants and Mount Olivets, stress on earnestness and reality was doubtless the intention. And as weapons of an aggressive proselytising religion, the Bible and its attendant tracts effectively dominated the chapel-goers' cultural field. Condescending in tone and instilling the virtue of keeping one's place, tracts were lavishly distributed, both at Sunday and day schools, as rewards for punctuality, diligence, decorum—and deloused heads. Fiction-reading, like theatre-going, was out of bounds during those first few decades of the century when Methodists most severely contracted the limits of their toleration. It seemed too dangerous for good Christians to expose themselves to the blandishments of imaginative literature—exercise of the imagination, which once deceived became itself the deceiver, unfitted the reader to meet the harsh realities of life. So for the working class and others the novel, with its continual display of human passions and feelings, was like Shakespeare banned—by the preachers and writers in the Wesleyan *Methodist Magazine*. In any case reading fiction was 'a waste of time' for those who believed that the grand object and condition of life itself was the prospect of heavenly bliss. Only long after Queen Victoria's accession were any secular books at all reviewed by the *Magazine*, whilst in the Methodist school of Woodhouse Grove, LEEDS, fiction was totally excluded from the library. Such attitudes limited the range and attractiveness of the literary experience available to the working class, when few other pleasures were possible, if they did not actually slow down the spread of reading itself. (The attitudes, incidentally, derived more from his followers than from Wesley's own example: he anthologised and simplified suitable poets and prose

M

writers to relieve 'the cultural narrowness of Methodist readers at no cost to their piety or morality'.)

⟨∞⟩

A list of the reward books 'suitable for Sunday School Prizes' published by Routledge includes the following, current about the turn of the century:

Wise and Otherwise	*Little Fishers and Their Nets*
Links in Rebecca's Life	*The Pocket Measure*
An Endless Chain	*The Master Hand*
Ruth Erskine's Crosses	*From Different Standpoints*
Mrs Solomon Smith Looking On	*A New Graft on the Family Tree*
Christie's Christmas	*Sidney Martin's Christmas*

PANSY BOOKS

⟨∞⟩

For what chapel folk lost in imaginative and intellectual range, they were offered compensation in a whole series of spiritual and social activities. From the Bright Hour and Sewing Circle, the Women's Guild to the Grand Bazaar, from the Sunday School and Band of Hope to the Youth Fellowship, from the Bible Study Group to the Men's Class and Leaders' Meeting, from the Anniversary to the annual Synod, there was involvement within the circle of the community and 'opportunity for the gratification of instincts denied expression elsewhere'. Chapel took a place now hardly filled by theatre, concert, cinema, ballroom and circulating library together. More recently the inclusion of secular concerts and home-produced operettas among the annual events has also helped to keep wandering youth within the fold and put a premium on local tenors or baritones with a repertoire of Gilbert and Sullivan, *The Quaker Girl* and *Bless the Bride*.

Liable at times to call themselves 'the salt of the earth', such congregations were like warm pockets of mutual comfort and esteem in the bleak surroundings of Coketown. Behind those somewhat forbidding façades—chapel buildings in Northern industrial towns often resembled mills (or mills resembled chapels)

—close in to the centre of the streets, or even in one or two places between HALIFAX and KEIGHLEY actually adjoining the factory, with its chimney shadow cast over the graveyard, anthems and enthusiasm and gaslight and tea urns steamed up the windows to shut in the faithful and shut out the world. Here were sources of consolation for the worker, and sedative or, if he chose to pursue it, inspiration in the struggle for social justice.

Chapel building went on apace. Pugin, in 1841, noted with irony that 'they are erected by men who ponder between a mortgage, a railroad or a chapel, as the best investment of their money, and who when they have resolved upon the persuasive eloquence of a cushion-thumping popular preacher, erect four walls with apertures for windows, cram the same full of seats which they readily let, and so greedy after self are these chapel-raiders that they form dry and spacious vaults underneath, which are soon occupied at a good rent by some wine and brandy merchant'. In many a Little Beulah, such as the one sketched by the mid-century novelist Mary Braddon, 'deal-and-plaster tabernacles furnished with an imitation mahogany pulpit, in form very much like a gigantic wine glass, and divided into small square pews, with narrow seats hewn out of the hardest wood he (the builder) could find in his yard', many a preacher such as Mr Joseph Slogood, Independent minister, sent the gruff thunder of a bass voice resounding out of the varnished wineglass, as he instructed or denounced his flock three times every Sunday, and banged the dust out of the flaring red velvet cushions. After the sermon, long, rambling, repetitive, his clerk, the apprentice of a neighbouring shoemaker, gave out 'homoeopathic doses of a long, lugubrious hymn'. And whereas Nonconformist men of business set their faces against the theatres, not only as 'over-exciting' but 'directly opposed to industry and close application' to work, they were able conscientiously to display their talents for fund-raising, organising, patronage and example-setting in the chapels, whose chief pillars they so often became.

The Church's impact on the industrial areas began with the 'slum parson' of early Victorian days. There came then a new insistence—shown in Blunt's *Duties of the Parish Priest* 1856—on the duty of the middle classes, lay and clerical, towards the labouring population. Richard Oastler, West Riding clothier and outstanding campaigner against child slavery in Yorkshire mills, left Methodism to join the established Church when he found that the Methodist mill-owners and stuff merchants were identifying their interests more and more with middle-class conservatism. Soup kitchens and clothing clubs were not enough; social reform on a radical basis was needed. In the campaign for the Ten Hours Bill, the meetings of the Short Time committees had vicars of parishes in LEEDS, BRADFORD, WAKEFIELD, HUDDERSFIELD, DEWSBURY, MANCHESTER in the chair, while Nonconformists, on the whole, opposed the Bill. 'It would curtail the rights of labour without permanently increasing its comforts. It would cost the poor too much, it would ultimately repay them nothing.' When the Bill became law and attempts were made to evade its provisions, churchmen from BRADFORD protested to the Queen. In this struggle the Church befriended the poor against the 'millocracy'; Dissent sided with the latter. Industry, self-control and getting-on came above the claims of the workman to a share in culture and leisure. 'He who plays as a boy will play when he is a man' Wesley had cautiously pronounced in disallowing time to spend on it. Methodists tended to be successful workmen, tradesmen, managers and employers who saw in other's poverty the consequences of disregard of this dictum.

One prevalent cause of earlier working-class indifference to the Church had been the distinction it made between rich and poor. Charging rent for pews was greatly resented. Yet the attempts of the Church Commissioners to intermingle the seats of poor and rich was made difficult by the objections of the latter, on whose pew rents the ministers' whole income depended. The Chartists led protests against what they called 'violation of the right of the people to their parish churches', in towns such as BOLTON, BLACKBURN, BRADFORD, MANCHESTER, NEWCASTLE, STOCKPORT. In BIRMINGHAM and the mining districts many who found both church and chapel cold and unsympathetic sought a better spirit of Christianity in the Chartist churches.

Wesley had stood out against the system of pew rents and refused to allow anyone, rich or poor, to call a particular seat his own. After his death the practice changed. By mid-century the distinction between the respectable and the common people was emphasised by pews and 'free seats' as much in chapel as in church. In 1849 a leading Wesleyan minister complained of chapels 'with expensive architectural frontispieces of stone and with interior ornaments of dead white and gold, where the poor's seats are like sheep pens, in the four corners of the building and behind the pulpit and where, even then, the seats adjoining are screened off most carefully by high rods and curtains'. Such apparent neglect of the poor was not only unbecoming, but detrimental to Methodism. Most of the newer chapels, in fact, had been built for the middle classes, and sprouted cupolas, rose windows, classical porches, Gothic tracery, in contrast to the old austere lines. In bad times the poor neglected to attend because they could not dress for it and were made to feel conspicuous beside those who could and did. In the great Northern towns, MANCHESTER and LEEDS, a French visitor, Léon Faucher, in 1845 found few of the working classes in the chapels; the operatives loitered at their doors or lounged at street corners until the hour of service was over and the public houses open.

⁘

Miss Dorothea Daniels—a social and religious (mainly religious) worker—besides her intimate knowledge of sin in our wretched city areas, was able to bring information of a world of wickedness beyond these. She was much horrified by extravagance, and especially by the extravagance of the working classes. The widest expansion of those large, sorrowful eyes came when she told in hushed tones what a fellow worker reported from MANCHESTER. 'Do you know, Miss Coupland says there are factory girls who actually have AS MUCH AS SIXPENCE every week to spend on sweets and their own idle pleasures!'

Introducing the Arnisons, a study of middle-class Nonconformist life,
Edward Thompson, 1935

This indeed was a logical result of Methodist training; industry and frugality produced riches, riches led to pride and love of the world. Unlike the rich man of the Bible, the rich man of this Puritan revival, who was not an idler enjoying himself while others toiled but an industrious and successful man making others richer by his industry, seemed able to step into both wealth and Paradise from the same ladder. 'God helps those who helps themselves.' (Compare HUDDERSFIELD'S motto, 'Juvat Impigros Deus'.) The consolation of the poor, in a world where wealth led to glory and poverty brought pity mingled with contempt, had to be that in the next world the soul of Dives would be no more esteemed than the soul of Lazarus—unless the fault lay in their own wickedness.

As the century advanced, some Methodist attitudes relaxed—towards reading, for instance, since games, concerts, plays, museum visits were out on the Sabbath and even oratorio, which commanded the passionate attachment of most Victorians, was allowed only on sufferance; but other kinds of intolerance stiffened, towards drink for example, and helped to fill the 'Blue Ribbon Army' with youthful recruits. While evangelicalism remained the religion of the home, its new rival, General Booth's Salvation Army, offered religion in the streets, conversion for the homeless and hungry, the drunkard and criminal, backed by social work and genuine care for their material conditions. The English Sunday, challenged by new scientific ideas from Darwin and by old continental ones, and also by the militant atheism preached to mass meetings of working men by Charles Bradlaugh in the 70s and 80s, slowly began to loosen its hold. The general change in the concept of religion from a 'public and documented system of beliefs, practices and aspirations' to a 'provision for personal needs' provided the loophole, for those who felt no such need themselves, to enjoy other weekend pleasures than family prayers, services and hymn singing. (How many homes, like that of the writer's grandparents, had a small harmonium in the sitting-room for this purpose, whereon the plangent rendering of *Sun of my soul, thou Saviour dear* already belongs to another age.) Even chapel felt the effects, although only slowly in such

staunch northern pockets of Nonconformity as the CALDER valley
or the communities on the Lancashire and Yorkshire border.

∽∾∾

A local preacher of the Calder Valley represents the remembered type. Thomas Midgley of Luddenden Dean, (1814-1897),
for sixty-three years served in the capacities of local preacher
and leader in the Hebden Bridge Circuit. The greatest epoch
of his life was when in March 1892 he had the honour of
preaching in City Road Chapel, London, founded by John
Wesley and a Mecca of his followers. Occupying the pulpit
where Wesley had stood, naturally he felt on his mettle, and
he chose his favourite text, 'For I am not ashamed of the
Gospel of Christ; for it is the power of God unto salvation to
every one that believeth'. It goes without saying that he
preached more eloquently than ever. He never tired of speaking of the event. He was assured that there he was fully appreciated; in his own country he often said 'a prophet hath no
honour'. . . . He was locally referred to as the 'Bishop of
Luddenden Dean'.

A Springtime Saunter Round and About Brontëland,
Whitely Turner, 1913

∽∾∾

A great deal had been done on the positive side to set in
balance against the negatives of the Nonconformists—directed
against Sabbath-breaking, theatre-going, drinking, gambling,
dancing, swearing and being worldly. 'Much of the moral, mental
and material improvement of the people was due to the work of
churches and chapels, Sunday schools and day schools, ragged
schools, town missions, temperance societies and thrift associations
—all adjuncts of religious bodies.' The *Official Guide* to BURNLEY
estimates that in 1900 the town had 25,000 Sunday-School
scholars, teachers and helpers out of a population of 97,000. Fifty
chapels and mission halls and ten churches were built during its
main period of population expansion—more than the number of
mills built. (There are now fifty-five places of worship altogether,
including those outside the Free Church Council.) Nonconformity,
it has been said, 'kept alive poetry and courage and an infinite
flow of kindliness from man to man'. Its message and its moral

discipline were as extravagant in their expression as had been the
dissolute manners against which the Methodist sect had risen in
revolt; and its way of life was conducted on a plane more suited
to simple, unthinking folk than to idea'd and questioning classes.
But from the turn of the century until after the First World War
many continued to find warmth, consolation and congenial busy-
ness in its fellowship meetings, evangelical crusades and constant
succession of 'do's'.

⟡

The Second Coming drew daily, hourly, nearer. John's spirit
shook within him when he heard these people called Methodists
sing of this. Listen!

> The dear tokens of His passion
> Still His dazzling body bears!
> Cause of endless exultation
> To his ransomed worshippers!
> With what rapture
> Gaze we on those glorious scars!

Do you mean to tell me that that is not poetry such as kills
the modish work that was its contemporary, the moment it is
set beside it?

Introducing the Arnisons, Edward Thompson, 1935

Hymns Ancient and Modern was by far the most popular volume
of verse in nineteenth-century England.

⟡

At the big brick chapel in SOUTH SHIELDS 'Harvest, Christmas
and Easter were the fixed and unalterable realities of our religion. . . . Our Sunday School festival, on the other hand, seemed a
forced and artificial affair. We, the Sunday School children, were
displayed on dizzy tiers round the altar in church . . . we had
lots of fluent little elocutionists whose self-confidence in public
amazed me. . . . The Chapel Bazaar, held in the Sunday School
hall was a brilliant affair. There were coloured lights, lanterns,
decorations, competitions, concerts and knife-and-fork teas and
suppers with solo songs and recitations. It was a grand do. . . .
There was a concert given by the sprightlier Sunday School
teachers and the less priggish members of the Christian Endeavour

Union. There were sketches, monologues, solos and dances, which I thought were extremely clever. . . . There was a tea stall at these do's, run by busy, pinafored chapel ladies wearing their best hats. Of course the tea was merely "hot and wet". . . . You could never depend on a good strong cup of tea at a Chapel Bazaar, even when they called it a "Grande Autumn Fayre" ' (James Kirkup). To children, in spite of hindsight about cause and effect, the annual picnic of the Wesleyan Bible Class was a red-letter event. 'Each year the power of God among us waxes in early June, to wane at the month's end. The graph of membership rose steeply, declined as sharply. The picnic was in mid-June' (Howard Spring).

A census taken in Yorkshire in 1901 showed that one city had a church for every 940 adults and just over a third of the population attended a place of worship on the census Sunday. In 1945, with one church for every 1,030 adults, the attendance had fallen by half. After the Second World War a similar census was taken. The total population had increased by 30,000 from the beginning of the century: there was still one church for every 1,137 adults. The attendance now amounted to thirteen per cent of the total population. This diminished group of congregations held an undue preponderance of the over-fifties and, in the chapels, nearly two-thirds of the attenders were women. Nonconformist Sunday Schools fared better in attendances than the Anglican—perhaps because their teaching dealt more with the substance of religion rather than the forms of worship and because many of the teachers taught also in day schools: but only ten per cent to twenty per cent of the scholars entered subsequently into chapel membership. For this and other reasons the relative position of Catholic churches had improved during the period. Ordinary people seemed to live their lives on broadly Christian principles, but without seeking any supernatural sanction for them. They were living on the spiritual capital of the past.

If they rationalise this change at all non-worshippers from the lower-middle and working classes give the impression that for them the Church is no longer relevant in a scientific age, being seen as subject to clerical domination and dogma. Clergy—whose

education and income no longer set them so far above skilled
artisans—are respected much less for their learning or their
personal qualities, whereas laymen prominent in church or chapel
affairs so often appear not to live up to the ideals they profess.
The average entrant to the ministry today falls markedly below
the standard reached in the past, as the churches acknowledge.

Whilst the minister is regarded as having a soft job—however
many exceptions there are to disprove it—churchgoers are
accounted either two-faced or privileged. 'Chapel is all right for
people with plenty of time' they say, or 'Can you pay the rates
with prayers?' Others find that 'The trouble with church people
is that they keep religion for Sunday' or that 'The nobs try to
make working folk believe in religion so that they won't kick up
a fuss'. Non-worshippers are also prone to detect hypocrisy in
others and then to take refuge in class-jealous attitudes: 'I spend
enough time on my knees scrubbing floors without kneeling on
Sundays'. The more honest criticism is simply 'Parsons are so
bad and the services so dull'. There may of course be expectation
of receiving without giving in the statement. 'When I had TB
and was off work for fourteen months I can tell you who looked
after me and the missus. It wasn't all those — people from chapel.
It was my mates from the boiler-shop. They'd sooner go to a pub
than to a church and so would I' (Seebohm Rowntree).

Another view :

At least one member of most families in the extended sense
of the word—perhaps an aunt or spinster cousin, if not a
parent—is likely to be a regular attender at church or chapel.
Church or chapel are still felt as in some sense a part of the
life of the neighbourhood. People will still speak of 'our chapel',
and many who do not normally attend will feel that an event
there is a neighbourhood event, and so go to an anniversary
service, or a bazaar, or a concert, or the start of the Whitsuntide walk, or the Christmas pantomime. . . .

For all that my impression is that even this limited sense of
belonging is weakening in most of the areas I know. Today,
most working class people go neither to church nor to chapel
except on special family occasions, once the parental order to

attend Sunday School has been withdrawn. In some places one of the recognised signs of becoming adult, together with going into long trousers for the boys or permission to use make-up for the girls, is this freedom to leave Sunday School and read the 'News of the World' at home like Dad.

The Uses of Literacy, Richard Hoggart, 1957

Freedom to do and say what one thinks and chooses on the Sabbath is a freedom still recent enough to be prized. The lack of real integrity among chapel and church-goers in Sunday profession and weekday practice can been seen more clearly under today's conditions. Pubs ('Satan's parlours') prove to be not wholly devoid of Christian spirit. Among the inheritors of a rural tradition where the squire and his lady knew all their tenants, went 'villaging', taught in school and dispensed charity without tracts, setting the example of the lessons they read, religious observance could more readily be kept alive. Among the factory employees of the great industrial cities, where 'paternalism' has little meaning and the State has swallowed up the functions of Lady Bountiful, while business men who attend church are suspected of social ambitions, observance might seem in danger of becoming a dead letter. After all if working-class families want the Sunday service they have only to switch on the radio; and many who protest that they are not 'church-going class' regularly do so—extra loud, as though enjoying their religion free of pressure and privilege—*and* they send their children to Sunday School so that dad can enjoy his afternoon sleep. (A survey conducted in DERBY in 1954 showed that sixty-three per cent of children between the ages of four and ten attended Sunday School and that fifty-six per cent between eleven and fifteen attended.)

FIGURES

If a chap knaws nowt but says nowt, fowk'll oft think he knaws summat.

Original Illuminated Clock Almanack, John Hartley, c. 1870

What's the poor miner's cocktail? (question in the '30s). A glass o' cauld watter wi' a scallion in.

Sorrows, Passions and Alarms, James Kirkup, 1959

The Industrial Revolution was really an industrial revelation which changed the faces of the North of England.

1066 and All That

'We are of the North, outwardly brusque, stoical, undemonstrative, scornful of the impulsive: inwardly all sentiment and crushed tenderness.' For 'crushed' read 'repressed'—no Northerner admits to being crushed in whole or part—and Arnold Bennett's statement of the general is fairly certain to find a good deal of particular application from Trent to Tyne.

Whether he is 'proud as Preston' or 'cocky as a tyke' the Northerner is likely in the company of visitors, especially those who think that by donning a cloth cap they're 'one of us', to close up still further. 'A gooid way to stop a chap's maath is to keep yer own shut.' He may be playing up to expectations in doing so, but consciousness of different traditions and a vastly different environment has made him cautious by nature. Historical notions of separatism between North and South have been reinforced by occupational separatism. In a twelfth-century poem, 'The Owl and the Nightingale', the nightingale expressed disgust at the idea of going North where men had such uncouth manners. In the fifteenth-century 'Second Shepherd's Play', Mak the Sheep

Stealer, adopting an imitation Southern accent as he pretends to be a king's yeoman, is recognised at once and told to 'take out that Sothren tothe'.

Making capital of the difference in temperament and environment, Mrs Gaskell called her story of troubled love between the daughter of a genteel New Forest parsonage and the hard-driving master of a cotton-mill, simply *North and South*. The South had come to seem soft and 'lah-di-dah'; today whenever bias ousts logic it tends to be rated as smug, over-privileged and under-productive. By contrast, whenever national newspaper or radio features look North they inevitably see craggy, square-cut, fiercely determined types, bluntly outspoken and interested only in winning, whether matches or contracts. With what justification?

The people are friendly enough, if you'll join them
In the Mecca Meat Market or the boozy clubs,
When you see the men at work as you walk through the cities
You think 'How wild, primitive, dirty and careless',
But when you talk to them in the pubs,
You find they like their jobs well enough,
Hand their wives money on a Friday
And respect the intellectual brother-in-law
Who is 'an accountant' or 'head of the costing department' :
Only the pox-bitten old reprobate, drunk in the corner
Hands us the scraps of profanity we need for our working class
    novel.
                                        The North, Brian Higgins

As an archetypal figure the mill-master deserves attention. He could be ruthless like one Luke Taylor, whose overlooker explained to the Committee on Artisans & Machinery (1824) that he was made to beat the child operatives when he failed to extract a certain quantity of work from them. He had seen the master himself with a horsewhip under his coat waiting at the top of the place, and when the children had come up he lashed them all the way into the mill if they were too late. The children had to come half a mile and be at the mill at five o'clock. Or he could be as respected as John Fielden of Todmorden, who worked up one-hundredth part of all the cotton imported into England and employed 2,000 persons. No man fought harder for a more humane life for factory workers, did more to relieve the pressure on children—whose daily work in following a spinning machine he found by practical tests involved not less than twenty miles of walking—or stated more clearly that the whole class of employers must be coerced in order to abate the evils of the system under which they grew rich. The factory workpeople of Lancashire erected a statue to Fielden in gratitude for espousing the Ten Hours Bill: he gave Todmorden its remarkable Grecian town-hall.

More representative of the early mill-master's spirit, and distinctly a good deal more articulate in its expression, was John Thornton, manufacturer of Milton, whose creed explains much of the difference between North and South. He began the hard way, earning a pittance in a draper's shop from which, by self-denial, he managed to save. He applied himself to obtaining a knowledge of goods and trade, despised indulgences and looked upon those who succumbed to them with contempt. He rose, not by luck but by effort, and believed that any working man could similarly raise himself to the power and position of a master. 'In fact everyone who rules himself to decency and sobriety of conduct and attention to his duties, comes over to our ranks; it may not always be as master, but as an overlooker, a cashier, a book-keeper, a clerk.'

He did not admire 'those whirligig characters that are full of this thing to day, to be utterly forgetful about it in their new interests tomorrow. Having many interests in life does not suit the life of a Milton manufacturer.' All his energies must bear on the fulfilment of one great desire—to hold a high place among the merchants of his country, the men of his town. Of course idle gentlemen and ladies were not likely to know much of a Milton manufacturer, unless he got into Parliament or married a lord's daughter.

Not a few Northern mill-masters did both—or earned their own title, like John Cunliffe of Addingham Low Mill, pioneer worsted spinner, whose grandson, Samuel Cunliffe Lister, developed the largest wool-combing firm in the world. He entered the House of Lords at Baron Masham after buying up an abbey estate and a couple of castles from members of the ancient aristocracy.

The main features of John Thornton are recognisable in many smaller figures—independent, 'hard men' of business, philistines, that first generation of manufacturers prepared to work like slaves and to live like slave-masters. Most of them had themselves been spinners, weavers, apprentices, schoolmasters, starting out with a minimum of capital, maximum of industry and enterprise. At first however much he hated the master, the ordinary workman was in personal touch with him and understood him. It was the steam engine, developing into a relentless power in the hands of an interested and avaricious master, to which young and old, employed and employer, were equally bound, that caused mills to become 'the iron bastilles of Manchester'. Mechanisation faced humane values in a conflict of forgone conclusions. In the second generation, when a manufacturer had been 'born in the cotton or the wool' the gulf between workman and employer grew wider and isolating. The axioms of trade (formulated by Pitt as 'wages and prices must be left to find their own level'), frantic commercial competition, the determination not to be beaten in any struggle between master and man, the feeling of growing power —all kept the gulf open and technical advance the criterion. Cromwell, said a mid-century critic, would have made a capital mill-owner.

For the children of the early industrial scene, at best pale, listless, thin, at worst stunted, diseased, degraded, a composite picture will serve best. The illustrations to Frances Trollope's *Life and Adventures of a Factory Boy* (1840) show ragged apprentices at

---

School: Grammar school, Wigan

School: Technical Institute, traditional

School: Mining and Technical College, modern

Chapel: Wesleyan Methodist chapel, Blackburn 1828

Chapel: (above) Circuit preacher

(left) Sion chapel, Burnley

Chapel: Sunday school walk

Chapel: Parish church, Wigan

Chapel: (left) Sherburn, Co Durham
(above) Barnsley. The old order

Chapel: The new

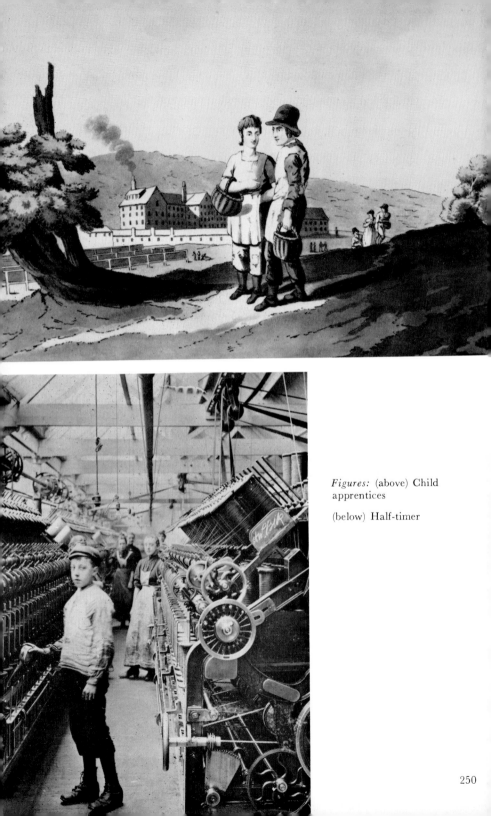

Figures: (above) Child apprentices

(below) Half-timer

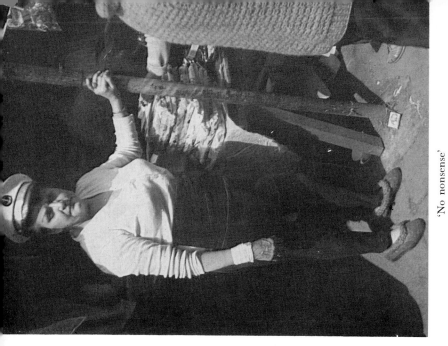

'No nonsense'

Figures: 'Rollers and Minis'

251

Figures: (above) 'Little Mester'; (below) Working partners

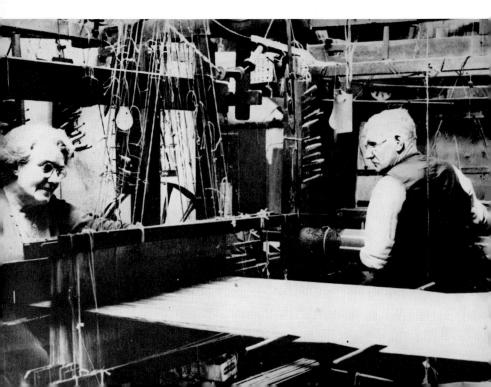

Figures: (left) Old timer
(below) A bit of leisure

Figures: Collier in control

Figures: Shields lasses

Figures: Looking ahead

their work in a textile mill and then in the farmyard that adjoins it, scrambling for extra food to supplement their ration of water porridge and oaten cake—at a pig trough. The picture of the mill, Deep Valley Mill, Derbyshire, was based on unimpeachable authority. It was certainly no worse than 'Hell Bay', a certain Mr Varley's mill, where for two months at a time children were worked from 5 am to 9 pm and for two nights in the week worked all night through as well. At other times children who had tended the machines by day crept into the beds left vacant by children who were to tend them through the night, or else lay down on the mill floor with a blanket to lie on and a horse cover to throw over them. The master of about 750 apprentices at a cotton mill at Blackburn stated that they 'developed into depraved characters'—although regulations said that boys and girls were to sleep in separate rooms and not more than two in a bed. They often tried to absent themselves from church-going on Sunday afternoon.

❧

When about six years of age I was sent to a cotton factory, and although I was of such tender age, I was treated there by the overlooker in a most brutal manner. I had only been a factory hand about four weeks when my mother, on washing me on the Sunday morning, was quite shocked to see the discolouration of my back as the result of a flogging I had received. I was then taken away from the factory and sent to a Dame's school, where I was taught to knit stockings.

Autobiography, John Wood, 1802-78

❧

Such children, picking up cotton waste, replacing bobbins or 'piecing' broken threads in temperatures ranging from $75°$ to $85°$ F, soon lost relish for their meals when dust and 'flue' choked their lungs; if spitting failed to expel it, emetics were given. Singing hymns to keep themselves from falling asleep at the machine —or tumbling in and being maimed for life; imploring parents and adults to tell them how many hours were still left to work; beaten with an iron stick known as the 'billy-roller'; deprived of open-air exercise; 'free' children and parish apprentices alike were treated worse than adult negro slaves. Perhaps their conduct *was* reprehensible: a fustian merchant declared that 'on a Sunday females often insult their well-behaved superiors in the streets, to such a degree that discreet gentlemen, even if they meet the factory people, will, if possible go on the other side of the street to avoid them'. *Noli me tangere* had replaced 'suffer little children . . .' in the ethos of the age. And at times when a weaver's wages sank to as little as 4s 6d a week, parish relief was refused for the family if he had children to send to the mill. However grieved the 'fustian-jackets', not all callous, felt at being unable to bring up their children at home, or having to put earning before schooling, they had other troubles to preoccupy them.

⟨∾⟩

Throughout the nineteenth century the burden of the factory system bore heavily on children in more ways than one. In 1904 the infant mortality rate of BURNLEY was 233 per 1,000, almost twice the rate at BURTON-ON-TRENT, for example. In his report the medical officer stated: 'BURNLEY is the largest textile manufacturing town in Europe, that is, it contains more looms for the weaving of cloth than any other town or city, and, as a larger number of women than men are employed in weaving, it follows that many infants are put out to nurse whilst the mothers are engaged in the weaving shed. When infants a few weeks old are thus put into the hands of unskilful nurses, it becomes certain that the food will be at times unsuitable, and the natural requirements of the infant not attended to. A sensible mother's care is necessary for the upbringing of a healthy child, and this motherly care cannot be obtained where mothers are extensively employed in factories. It need excite no surprise, then, that in manufacturing towns the infant mortality is large, very much greater than in non-textile towns where mothers usually nurse their own children and are not compelled to put them out to nurse'.

	Infant mortality rate 1890-1905	Percentage of women occupied between ages 15 and 35	
		Total	Married or widowed
BURNLEY	208	90.9	59.7
PRESTON	208	89.4	50.5
BLACKBURN	183	91.8	63.9

NOTTINGHAM	180	84.6	27.5
OLDHAM	170	87.3	33.4
BOLTON	166	87.4	24.7
BURY	164	88.9	44.8

ᘛᘚ

'Fustian' became the traditional workman's dress during the early nineteenth century, in contrast to the 'broadcloth' of the middle classes, both wool and linen having practically disappeared from the wardrobe of factory hands. Men's shirts were made of bleached or coloured cotton cloth, women wore printed cottons; woollen petticoats were seldom to be seen on the washing line. All working men wore hats, round, cone-shaped, cylindrical, broad-brimmed or brimless: anyone not possessing a hat made himself a low, four-cornered cap out of paper. Their clothes were thick, stiff and heavy but did not keep out the cold as well as woollens could do. After the sweating heat of the factory the workers faced wind and wet without the flannel vest, cummerbund and flannel scarf common to the broadcloth class.

Stephen Blackpool was one of the fustian-jackets, a powerloom weaver and good worker; 'a rather stooping man, with a knitted brow, a pondering expression of face and a hard-looking head sufficiently capacious, on which his iron-grey hair lay long and thin; forty years of age; he looked older, but he had had a hard life'. After the lights were out in the great factories, which seemed when illuminated like fairy palaces—or so the travellers by express train said—and the bells had rung for knocking off for the night, he stood in the street 'with the old sensation which the stoppage of the machinery always produced—the sensation of its having worked and stopped in his own head'. The nervous strain of watching and working with machinery aged these men faster than the heaviest physical exertion.

These are the working-class archetypes, man and boy. In some respects the last hundred years have not produced any great change. A retired female 'drawer', talking recently to the writer about her working day in a silk-spinning mill, recurred again and again to the numbing din of the wheels, flapping belts and machines, and its relentless continuance from the red starting light at 7.45 am to the cleaning-up light at 4.55 pm. Her whole day was spent standing; a half-hour 'dinner break' only just allowed her to go home, except on Fridays when she had to queue for wages during the first quarter of that half-hour. The machinery 'caught' her once, when the overlooker had not attended it and it 'fed back'. (But the sense of class difference between mill-worker and, say, shop assistant, has steadily faded with the fading of the 'clog and shawl' era. Wages, conditions and cheap fashions now permit all alike to go to work indistinguishably up-to-the-moment in dress.)

Stephen Blackpool was one of the hundreds of thousands of workers whose whole condition of life suffered depreciation under the factory system, in which fierce competition and pursuit of wealth consumed human material as never before and in which rising out of the ruck required formidable energy and self-discipline. He was not one of 'those remarkable Hands, who piecing together their broken intervals of leisure through many years had mastered difficult sciences and acquired a knowledge of most unlikely things. He held no station among the Hands who could make speeches and carry on debates.' Yet, amid all the deterrent conditions, the figure of the self-educated working-man stands out, sometimes with a name still remembered locally. Engels heard working men 'whose fustian jackets hardly held together, speak with great knowledge on botany and astronomy'.

In Lancashire and the West Riding workmen naturalists were familiar figures : some formed important collections of fossils, insects, plants and mosses. One of the founders of Todmorden Botanical Society (1852) was a 'twister' and specialist in local mosses; at Hebden Bridge a whitesmith discovered a new fossil shell and established a private museum. In the neighbourhood of Oldham there were 'common handloom weavers, who throw the shuttle with unceasing sound, though Newton's *Principia* lies open on the loom, to be snatched at in work hours, revelled over in meal times or at night'. Artisan poets revealed the workman's inner feelings and aspirations also : among these were Samuel Bamford, porter in a calico-printing works, Joseph Skipsey, who

managed to compose poetry by chalking on the mine trap-door
he tended, John Nicolson and George Linnaeus (good botanical
agnomen) Banks. Their verses appeared in local newspapers and
almanacks—another characteristic production of the district—
such as *Hartley's Original Clock Almanack* (first published 1865),
Halifax Illuminated Clock Almanack, Barnsley's *Bag o' Shoddy
Almanack*, Pudsey's *The Weyver's Awn Comic Almanack* or
Sheffield's *Wheelswark Chronicle*, where dialect items with many
'a bit o' serious reasonin' lapt up in a bit o' nonsense' had a long
and popular appeal. Sometimes the work of such poets was collected and published by local subscription : their talents may not
have been great but their spirit sang.

LINES

ON FINDING A BUTTERFLY IN A WEAVING SHED.

Nay, surelee tha's made a mistak;
    Tha'rt aght o' thi element here;
Tha may weel goa an' peark up o'th' thack,
    Thi bonny wings shakin' wi fear.

Aw should think 'at theease rattlin' looms
    Saand queer sooart o' music to thee;
An' tha'll hardly quite relish th' perfumes
    O' miln-grease, —what th' quality be.

Maybe' tha'rt disgusted wi' us,
    An' thinks we're a low offald set
But tha'rt sadly mistaen if tha does,
    For ther's hooap an' ther's pride in us yet.

Tha wor nobbut a worm once thisen,
    An' as humble as humble could be;
An' tho we nah are like tha wor then,
    We may yet be as nobby as thee....

Hartley's Yorkshire Ditties

Among those 'hands' who could make speeches and carry on
debates, and who saw the only chance of betterment for their
class in the study and pursuit of politics were figures who became

nationally known—Ebenezer Elliott, the corn-law rhymer; John Doherty, cotton-spinner from Ulster and founder of the strongest trade union of his day, who edited two papers for working-men, *The Poor Man's Advocate* and *The Voice of The People*. Belief in the power of the press was pathetically keen among miners and millworkers : so much so that whole factory populations met the London coach that brought Cobbett's *Register* to Lancashire towns. Most successful of all democratic papers was *The Northern Star* run by Feargus O'Connor, a powerful orator in the cause of Chartism. To these spokesmen and to the unstamped pamphlets and papers produced in Manchester, Leeds and Bradford, working men looked for their intellectual as well as material progress.

When conditions were beginning to change in their favour the miner and the weaver showed their mettle in other fields. Football gradually replaced rougher sports such as cock-fighting, 'purring' (a kicking match in Lancashire), bare-knuckle boxing. Its progress in the North, with working men on their Saturday afternoons off taking relaxation on any public recreation ground, at first went almost unnoticed by the dominant Southern teams. Blackburn Rovers formed in 1874; Bolton Wanderers began, without any funds, each member of the team subscribing 6d to pay for the ball; at their first match Aston Villa's gate receipts totalled 5s 3d. A few years later, when the South realised that a Northern team had got into the FA Cup Final against the Old Etonians, it was the Etonians who scored the only goal. In 1883, however, Blackburn Olympic met the Old Etonians for Final honours. The Blackburn team consisted of a cotton operative, a plumber, an iron-moulder's dresser, a spinner, three weavers, a picture-frame maker, a dentist's assistant and two Sheffield workmen. They were twenty-one pounds lighter and two or three inches shorter, man for man, than their opponents, but the result was a portent : the Etonians lost by two goals to one. Blackburn Olympic took the cup North—the first football-hero figures of their class and forerunners of a type who were to turn professional and make football the serious business of the talented poor.

The successful footballer, one who 'makes a science of it', has a special place in the gallery of Northern personalities. His combination of physical gifts with application and cunning in the use of them is respected and admired. In Rugby League the home team of ex-miners or heavy steel workers is spoken of with the genuine pride implied in 'our lads'. As in Lancashire League cricket, whole towns are, or were, involved in the team's performance; today, with a widening cultural climate, the concentration of support has thinned.

The local loyalties and the caustic wit of the Northerner had unrivalled scope on the sports ground where the working man could appeal to a massed audience of his fellows. The classic story of the Southern spectator watching a Yorkshire and Lancashire match displays the loyalty at its fiercest. 'Well played,' he shouted. To his right a hand withdrew a stubby pipe and a voice, asked : 'Art 'a Yorkshire, lad?' 'No.' To the left another pipe was taken out and a more suspicious voice enquired : 'Art 'a Lancashire, lad?' 'No.' 'Then,' came both rasping voices together, 'what's it got to do with thee?' Spectator participation is a skilled art. The barracker on his home ground has always been a figure to reckon with in Northern cricket circles and nowhere more than in the Barnsley League, where bat and miner's pick are wielded by the same hand, often above and below the same space of ground. Barrackers' wit has had a real part in keeping the game alive or cutting 'heroes' down to size. Every club used to have at least one self-appointed scourge of his own and the visiting teams. When the Barnsley team itself on one occasion faced a large score on a very wet wicket, the captain decided to play for a draw and to achieve it by wasting as much time as possible. After every ball he walked down the wicket and indulged in extensive 'gardening' : not merely tapping the divots back but thumping them in with resounding thuds. One such episode and slow return to crease caused the club critic to bellow 'Ayup : tha wants to be careful with all that thumpin' : there's men workin' under theer.'

Arnold Bennett noted the fact that one could always distinguish miners from potters on their way to early morning work. Potters would whistle on the way, miners never. No one ever named a pub 'The Jolly Miners' like Etruria's 'Jolly Potters'. The reason is cut into the cast-iron tombstone at MADELEY, near Coalbrookdale, which stands over the separate cast-iron gravestones of nine 'men', aged between twelve and thirty-seven years,

> Who were killed by the unhooking of the chains
> In which they were ascending the shaft of the
> Brick kiln Leasow Crawstone Pit in this parish
> At the end of their day's labour on Thursday the 27 September 1864.

It is underlined by George Orwell in his account of the 'dataller' (a miner who attends to pit roofing) who was twice buried and twice partially freed in the same accident, before being buried for good by a third fall of roof. His mates learnt afterwards that he had taken to kissing his wife before he went to work—a thing he had not done for over twenty years—because he knew that the place was unsafe.

Before the era of motor-bike, service bus, cinema, TV and juke-box, miners were almost a race apart, aloof from other workers in the enclosed communities of the pit villages. With split shifts and night shifts, they had to live close by—as did dockworkers and ironworkers in the North East and North West--and this made for continuity of social contacts between work and leisure.

They lived with the extra tension brought by danger and by tough physical conditions. Their ways were as rough as their boots and black faces: they had ready fists, a passion for pigeons and whippet-racing, fierce enthusiasm at cricket and football and unquestioned mastery in their households. To travel on foot through a mining district near DONCASTER, as the writer recalls doing in the early 30s, and to see the unemployed men squatting on their heels at street corners—'hunker parliaments'—a slender racing-dog between their knees, was to feel like a trespasser. The idea that colliers don't give a serious thought to a thing—save Doncaster races (D. H. Lawrence's view)—seemed irrelevant to these bowed, pensive figures: though in good times, if the incomer wants to approach them at ease, there is perhaps no better place than a St Leger meeting.

The miner is still a conspicuous figure, even away from work. Standing near the cross-roads, say at SHERBURN-IN-ELMET, feet strongly planted apart, his boots, ankle-gaiters, dark trousers, broad leather belt, open-necked shirt, loose jacket and broad shoulders, his stocky build, slightly bandy legs, pugnacious features and hint of beard make him as noticeable as the splendid Alsatian he holds on lead. The difference in bearing is marked, however, if one goes from the old brick miners' village of SHOTTON and EASINGTON, Co Durham, with their clubs for mining officials and for working men, their wooden social halls and seats round the First World War memorial, to PETERLEE. Here in the townscape of shopping precincts and open greens, of glass, concrete and featured trees, with houses designed in decoratively austere wood and white-painted shapes by Victor Pasmore, it is the miner who seems to be the intruder.

Peter Lee—whose work for DURHAM miners is commemorated in Peterlee—began work at nine years old in a Lancashire cotton mill; at ten he became a 'pit laddie' in Durham; before reaching seventeen he was a hewer at the coal face. Later he served for many years as a 'check-weighman', a county councillor and a member of Durham Miners' Association executive. He was a local preacher and strong Primitive Methodist. He typified the courage, integrity and humanity of the mining community he served, as Primitive Methodism, the great educative force of the northern miner, stood for peaceful, progressive Christian democracy.

Experience of hard times, and inherited memories of harder, breed odd quirks in human nature. In a household that the writer knew well, one of two spinster sisters was employed, after she had finally given up working in the woollen mill, as weekly help for cleaning and washing. 'Martha the mender' was always dressed in cast-off coats and hats, or in ancient rusty black for Sunday; she never bought a pair of shoes, stockings or a newspaper if one could be handed down to her. Hardly ever failing to turn up for Monday's wash or Friday's clean, winter and summer, when well over seventy, she seemed in need of the few shillings so earned. She and her sister were always saving against the time when both were past work. They lived in a one-room-up, one-room-down cottage in a back street overshadowed by the mill. In cold weather a coat, too old even for their wear, was the extra blanket on their bed; in summer, for a holiday, they went a ride or two to the end of the trolley-bus route and sat in the park. When she died, aged eighty, Martha's sister received her savings. A year later the sister died too and a niece 'who'd never been near them' inherited the money : it amounted to over £9,000.

George Orwell in the 30s remarked on the anomaly that even in times of depression, the dole and PAC, people in Wigan did not always lower their standards by cutting out luxuries and concentrating on necessities, but often the other way about. Unlike Martha, those really on the poverty line kept up their spirits by the cheap luxuries increasingly available—hire-purchase clothes, fish-and-chips and flutters on the pools. Orwell regarded it as a psychological adjustment by the working class, not as a subtle means supplied by their rulers to avert revolution. ('Keeping your pecker up' is a deeply ingrained Northern habit.)

Thirty years later solid wages, endless cigarettes and TV, the firm's outing to Skegness or Southport, have given at least the hallucination of wellbeing to the majority—a state reflected by the deportment of the young. The teenage girl now enjoys her brief, butterfly flight of dress, dance, hair-dos and cinema, whatever her background. The young man has his motor-bike, fishing-rod, transistor set and drape suit—or whatever clothes mass-fashion decrees and cheapens—as well as beer and skittles at his 'supporters' club'. He is in distant line with the 'swells' and 'mashers' of music-hall : his model and the girls' idol is the 'pop' star. This hero-figure of the times is himself, as a rule, a working-class boy, of provincial and industrial background, who has come out of the clubs and 'groups' of Newcastle, Liverpool or Manchester by the vertical escape ladder to the heights of classless affluence.

The other side to the picture of providence and penny-savers and pop-cult can be found in the description of Leddersford Conservative Club—'the place where money grew: with its ten guinea annual subscription plus incidentals it was for rich men only'. 'Here was the place where decisions were taken, deals made between soup and sweet; here was the place where the right word or smile or gesture could transport one into a higher grade over-night' (*Room at the Top*). The bar is usually crowded with business men 'slaving to help the export drive': not all of them speak standard English: since Leddersford's main manufacture is textiles most have received their higher education from the Technical College, where they've rubbed shoulders with the com-mon people and picked up traces of a Northern accent. What marks the users of the bar as rich is their size, their suits, their double whiskies, gold cigarette cases and talk of holidays in Majorca, and their confidence—the confidence that comes from being boss of the works, or the sons of fathers who are.

The Leddersford atmosphere is loaded no doubt by novelist's licence. A composite portrait of a member of the club and of a leader of the textile industry in real life would read more com-monly like this:

'Educated at the local grammar school, where his sporting achievements brought him more fame than his academic.

Served his apprenticeship at L—— Bros. After completing his course at the Technical College he founded, at the age of only 22, along with his brother, the firm of M—— & N—— Ltd, English wool merchants.

He also found time to play cricket, opening the innings for his club, and rugby football and golf, which he still plays. During the war he commanded a company of Home Guards, a post which he continues to hold.

In the last ten years has been chairman of the Fleece Com-mittee, member of the executive committee of the Chamber of Commerce and President of the Wool Federation. He is a JP, ex-chairman of his school Governors, prominent in the activities of the local Conservative Party and acts as judge at the great Shire Show. He is also a keen churchman. His business is now a sub-sidiary company of the County Woollen Combine Ltd, of which he is a director.'

Men like this have not as much time for double whiskies at the club as might be supposed. They come in the line of Mr Rounce-well—'a little over fifty perhaps, of a good figure, with a clear voice, a broad forehead from which his dark hair has retired, a shrewd though open face : a responsible-looking gentleman dressed in black, portly enough, but strong and active, with a perfectly natural and easy air'—whom Dickens portrays as the iron-master, active at election times, a good speaker, plain and emphatic, able to carry all before him in the business part of the proceedings. Mr Rouncewell had been an apprentice, had lived on workman's wages, married a foreman's daughter and beyond a certain point had had to educate himself. If he had any extrava-gance it was in the education of his daughters 'to make them worthy of any station', a weakness shared by his modern coevals who give their sons a university education—though not usually for matrimonial reasons.

❧

The lines on the face of an old working-class woman are often magnificently expressive—but they are hard earned. . . . It is often a face with a scaly texture and the lines, looked at closely, have grime in them; the hands are bony claws covered with densely lined skin, and again the dirt is well ingrained there : years of snatched washes, usually in cold water have caused that. The face has two marked lines of force—from the sides of the nose down to the compressed lips; they tell of years of 'calculating'. Many old working-class women have an habitual gesture which illuminates their life behind : . . . a rhythmic smoothing of the hand down the chair-arm, as though to smooth everything out and make it workable : in others there is a working of the lips or a steady rocking. None of them could be called neurotic gestures, nor are they symp-toms of acute fear; they help the constant calculation.

The Uses of Literacy, Richard Hoggart, 1957

Let's aal gan tiv Alice's hoose,
Alice's hoose is like a palace is Alice's hoose !
There's carpets on the floor, a knocker on the door,
Aa've nivver seen sae many people knock on a door afore !

❧

The ironic comment on poverty in this Tyneside jingle also emphatically places the most important figure in the house— Alice. The continued Northern tradition that so many women go out to work, and for only about half the money the men get, does not alter the fact that their pride remains in the home. There is indeed a double pride : household economics depend on the woman's weekly wage packet (and no doubt will do so as long as income per head remains eighteen per cent lower in the North than in the South East), and yet houses are still kept like miniature palaces. The polished cleanliness, the crisp washing of clothes, the meticulous curtains and doorsteps, the home cooking—bread, pastry, cake, puddings—speak for themselves. The woman also expects to uphold standards in the home, to manage the money—she can even be seen paying her husband's bus fare—and to run the family 'dos' and anniversaries. A Christmas 'do' in a retired weaver's two-room cottage with about twenty people present, including in-laws, intendeds, sons and grandchildren, a roaring fire against the freezing wind and relays of 'high tea', still stir the writer's memory. Amidst all this the woman finds time to help needy causes; her warm-heartedness is a byword. 'If the foreigner makes good any claim on their latent kindliness and hospitality, they are faithful and generous and thoroughly to be relied on' : the character given by Mrs Gaskell to people in the Haworth district applies pretty well to the Northern housewife in general. So does 'dwellers among them must be prepared also for certain uncomplimentary, though most likely true observations, pithily expressed. The affections are strong and their foundations lie deep : but they are not—such affections seldom are—widespreading : nor do they show themselves on the surface.'

∽⌇∾

THE MANAGER

Mrs M. whose husband has worked for the same employers for thirty years governed her house with the skill of a born administrator. Her two eldest daughters were working in linen-drapers' shops and she did all the housework herself, arranged day by day with regularity and method. On Monday she brushed all the Sunday clothes, folded them up and put them away; on

Tuesday she swept thoroughly upstairs, Wednesday, she did
the week's washing, Thursday she ironed, Friday she baked and
'black-leaded', and on Saturday she cleaned the lower part
of the house, kitchens etc., and did most of the cooking for
Sunday. On Sunday all was ready for a day of leisure and
comfort. The result of having a wife of this kind at the head
of the house is that the husband after he comes home from
work, seldom stirs out of the house again. . . . Whenever a man
says that he does not 'care to turn out again' one may be sure
that the wife understands how to make things comfortable for
him.

At the Works, Lady Bell, 1907

The reasons then for the conceptual difference between Southern
and Northern English are pretty plain : to do more than survive
in the industrial growth areas of the nineteenth century meant
subordinating almost all else to the effort. If one had to isolate
the most general feature of the result, without regard to the finer
shadings of difference between Northerners themselves, it would
perhaps narrow down to the conclusion that force of character
has prevailed in the North at the expense of 'form', in the
cherished Southern sense. Furthermore actions always are rated
there higher than words, a truism but a guide to conduct not
necessarily appreciated elsewhere. When it comes to words, 'saying
what one means and meaning what one says' has become a rather
self-conscious Northern trait.

To live there did not mean to like those towns
Of bleak black streets that herringboned the hills,
Those valleys choked with railways, roads, canals,
Dark rivers full of suds, where lorries roared
And every clough that carved its way through grit
Had mill, forge, dam for adit or exit.

To live with did not mean to like those spires
Of huge stone chapels, steel-hooped chimney stacks,
Grim sentinels set round the orthodox,
With bird-limed bust, soot-gathering in the square

For those who knuckled down and never lifted view
From workbench, boardroom, council-chamber, pew.

To leave them did not mean that liking changed
By less or more . . . but sweetest Auburn's green
Though pleasing still, soon palled, and stately queens
Of other shires, as if by soot's revenge,
Seemed pale, blank towns, whose vacant faces proved
How liking had been undermined by love.

∽♥∽

Among the figures who have emerged from the industrial
scene into public gaze somewhat larger than life and twice as
vigorous, the 'Cards' and the powerful aldermen, the women
MPs and the Union leaders, the choirmasters and contraltos, the
philanthropic magnates and the famous cricketers, one figure is
seldom conspicuous to the generality, yet pre-eminent for the
part he has played in shaping the whole Northern scene. The
engineer, from Arkwright and Crompton, Hargreaves and Kay,
Stephenson and Watt, Bramah and Maudslay, Nasmyth and
Whitworth, through a whole host of lesser names and minor inventors, has alone made the progressive course of industry possible. He is the creative technician par excellence : to him it is
the problems of harnessed power and production, offering a continual challenge, that count, not those that production leaves in its
train or the sort of society it promotes.

'An inventor cannot just arrange things in industry as he would
like them to be—existing factors will determine the use of his invention . . . (When) I first thought of a device (1938) which would
detect thickness variations in slivers, I was a woolcomber and I
was taught—not very successfully—how to feel these variations
by hand and by weighing. It was this lack of success which led
me to devise and make a simple wheel and groove through which
the sliver ran, the wheel feeling the changes in the thickness. A
pen and strip-paper recorder were added : this showed variations
as a graph. I felt this was not enough and began to think of ways
of coupling it to a gill-box so that the thickness variations would
themselves vary the draft as required to produce a level sliver. . . .

The delayed action mechanism is the crux of the Auto-leveller, this and all other associated problems being solved about 1949 when I made the first practicable machine in my workshop'. One more production problem solved: by 1954 over one thousand of these Auto-leveller units were in commercial operation.

The stages in the process of taking tasks away from the slowness or uncertainty of hand and eye to the speed and near perfectibility of the machine—pass more rapidly nowadays than in the dying days of the hand-loom. 'An unconscionable time in dying' its historian said. A West Riding handloom weaver is on record as making his weekly piece of high-grade cloth in an upper room of his home for thirty years, up to his fortieth birthday in 1880. By that year the power loom was able to produce as good a fabric as the older loom, and the cost advantages enjoyed by the domestic handloom—no wear and tear costs to be met by the employer, no bill for power or floor space rent, no foreman's or loom-tuner's wages and other etceteras—had been wiped out, but only after the power-loom's existence for more than fifty years. Our weaver's employer, having erected a powerloom shed, told him that no more yarn would be put out to him and offered him a job in the new shed. 'And who else'll be working there? Lasses! work wi't lasses? Not me.' So he came home, chopped up his loom for kindling wood, rented a bit of land and spent the next forty years growing red cabbages for Leeds and Bradford markets. A characteristic bit of Northern 'cussedness' and independence.

The history of Northern industry is studded with the names of inspired mechanics, like Isaac Holden whose invention of new combing machinery induced Samuel Cunliffe Lister (Baron Masham) to take out a joint patent with him and eventually brought the former weaver's drawboy to a knighthood. Or like that of the founder of a Huddersfield firm which in 1860 employed two workpeople and specialised in the design and manufacture of one product, wooden patterns for cast iron gear wheels. Today the organisation, still centred on Huddersfield,[1] comprises an engineering combine employing over ten thousand people;

[1] In 1961 one of the manufacturing plants was moved to Sunderland and has played an important part in NE economic redevelopment since.

its products cover an engineering field which ranges from gears, gear-cutting plant, steel and bronze castings and precision tools to agricultural tractors and implements, industrial tractors and earth-moving equipment, and two makes of high quality sports cars. Mining engineers and oilfield technicians from Africa and Australia, Canada and South America are familiar with the firm's specialised units. Gear manufacture formed the basis of this extensive organisation : the rear axle of every trolley bus built in Britain incorporates a worm gear drive based on a design pioneered by the company, and the world's leading shipbuilders use its turbine gear-cutting machines. The present chairman bears the same name as his grandfather who founded the company. Such men have known what they were about and spared no effort to achieve it.

Any selection of figures of industrial England ought in justice to include machines.

> We can pull and haul and push and lift and drive,
> We can print and plough and weave and heat and light,
> We can run and jump and swim and fly and dive,
> We can see and hear and count and read and write. . . .

Since Kipling wrote the machines have more than kept pace with his visionary words : they have almost taken over. Now not only the Auto-leveller, the automatic Embroidery Machine, the automatic Flatwork (laundry) Folder, but 'ROLF'—the Remotely Operated Longwall Face coal cutter and loader, the Auto-setter for shaping nylon knitted garments, the multi-colour Automatic Worsted Loom, computer control of pneumatic and electronic equipment of all kinds 'serve us four-and-twenty hours a day'. The engineer who knows the secret of the machine is approaching an innings of almost two centuries. His expertise is respected everywhere : most problems from the spatial and social organisation of factories to the control of traffic and siting of airports come back to him. If he remains largely anonymous it is not because his creations have left no imprint. His signature is written in characters too sprawling almost to read over both the North of England and, incidentally, much of the rest of the world. Few since the mysterious

O

'General Ludd' have challenged its significance : to do so now in the North would be apostasy. Only a Lewis Mumford, concerned with the whole history and culture of cities, discards blinkers to place the 'myth of the machine' and the primacy of technology in clear relation to our social order, its built-in problems and its still human figures.

AUTHORITIES CONSULTED

The following works are chief among those to which reference has been made.

Allen, G. C., *British Industries and their Organisation*

Altick, R. D., *The English Common Reader*

Backus, N., *Methodism and the Struggle of the Working Classes*

Bryant, Sir Arthur, *English Saga, 1840-1940*

Dury, G. H., *The British Isles: a Systematic and Regional Geography*

Engels, F., *The Condition of the Working Class in England* (ed Henderson and Chaloner)

Ensor, R. C. K., *England 1870-1914* (Oxford History of England)

Evans, Joan, *The Victorians*

Hammond, J. L. and B., *The Bleak Age*

Hammond, J. L. and B., *The Town Labourer*

Harrison, J. F. C., *Learning and Living, 1790-1960*

Hill, C. P., *British Economic and Social History, 1700-1939*

Hoggart, R., *The Uses of Literacy*

Howarth, P., *The Year is 1851*

Jervis, F. R. J., *The Evolution of Modern Industry*

Jones, G. P. and Pool, A. G., *100 Years of Economic Development in Great Britain, 1840-1940*

Knowles, K. G. J. C., *Strikes*

Martin, G., *The Town*

Montgomery, J., *The Fifties*

Moorhouse, G., *Britain in the Sixties*

Orwell, G., *The Road to Wigan Pier*

Rowntree, B. Seebohm and Lavers, G. R., *English Life and Leisure*

Smailes, A. E., *North England*

Trevelyan, G. M., *English Social History*

Trevelyan, G. M., *British History in the Nineteenth Century and After, 1782-1919*

'Truscot, Bruce', *The Redbrick University*

Wigham, E. L., *Trade Unions*

*

Bradford Textile Society *Journals*, 1949-66

British Association papers, 'Manchester and its Region', 1962

HMSO, *The Deeplish Study on Improvement Possibilities in a District of Rochdale*, 1966

INDEX

Page numbers in *italic* type refer to illustrations

VIEW NORTH

This book comes from the same stable as a wide range of new books and also of reprints of classics of the past about the north of England, with particular emphasis on its work and life.

New books currently in print include Arthur Raistrick's **Old Yorkshire Dales**, J. Allan Patmore's **Railway History in Pictures: North-West England**, K. Hoole's **Regional Railway History volume 4: North-East England** and Baron Duckham's **The Yorkshire Ouse.** To be published within a few months of the appearance of **View North** are Owen Ashmore's **Industrial Archaeology of Lancashire** and Frank Nixon's **Industrial Archaeology of Derbyshire.** Also in active preparation are two further volumes in the Railway History series covering Lancashire and the West Riding of Yorkshire, and two volumes in the Canals of the British Isles series, covering the Canals of North-West England and the Canals of North-East England.

Reprints currently in the list include **Tomlinson's North Eastern Railway, Tomlinson's Comprehensive Guide to Northumberland,** Aikin's **A Description of the Country from Thirty to Forty Miles Round Manchester, Baines's Lancashire**, a reprint of the directory in two volumes, while very soon after the appearance of **View North** the list will also include **Miss Weeton's Journal of a Governess** in two volumes, rich in social and economic comments on Lancashire in the early years of the nineteenth century.